Eisenhower and Berlin, 1945

THE NORTON ESSAYS IN AMERICAN HISTORY
Under the general editorship of
HAROLD M. HYMAN

William P. Hobby Professor of American History
Rice University

Eisenhower and Berlin, 1945

The Decision to Halt at the Elbe

Stephen E. Ambrose

W · W · NORTON & COMPANY

New York · London

SBN 393 09730-7

Library of Congress Catalog Card No. 67-15818

For Judy, with love

Contents

MAPS

Foreword

MANY PEOPLE in the West today believe that it was possible for the Anglo-American forces to beat the Russians to Berlin in April, 1945, and capture the city. They also feel that had the West done so some great advantages would have accrued.

One man was responsible for the failure to try—General Dwight David Eisenhower. This essay is an attempt to understand his decision to stop his forces at the Elbe River and leave Berlin to the Red Army. What he did, why he did it, and what the results were—these questions are my primary concern.

No one has yet explained in any detail exactly what advantages the West would have gained had Eisenhower captured Berlin. Those who write on or talk about the subject concentrate on the day-to-day details of operations in April, assuming that the capture of Berlin by one side or the other made a tremendous difference. Since they never say what the difference would have been, one must ask, "What did it all matter?"

Any answer must be conjecture, but it can be based on knowledge of what did happen. After V-E Day neither side raised any question about the occupation zones that had been created months before the war ended, and the West gave up those parts of Germany allotted to the Russians that Eisenhower's armies had overrun. The Russians did the same for the West; within eight weeks of the end of the war American, British, and French troops were in Berlin. Apart from the matter of written agreements, almost everyone wanted to try and keep the war-time alliance alive, even if only on their own terms. In May, 1945, neither side was ready to risk World War III.

In the case of the Berlin question there are numerous myths which serve to confuse the problem. Those that find their way into print, such as the assertion that Eisenhower could have breezed into Berlin had he wanted to or that the "National Redoubt" played the major role in his thinking, are comparatively easy to deal with. This is not the case with those myths that are never written down but are part of the common remembrance. These stories, precisely because they never appear in print, are extremely tenacious.

The major myth in regard to Berlin is that if the Americans had captured the city they would have held it and there would be no Berlin problem today. This is patently nonsense. Nothing of the kind would ever have happened. But by refusing to state frankly what difference an American capture of Berlin would have made, while treating the decision as of about the same importance as the Emancipation Proclamation, Eisenhower's critics can count on their readers to assume that it made a great difference—that in fact the West would have held the city.

It is impossible to work out the origins of the myth. I have never seen it in print. Yet nearly everyone to whom I talk, be he a veteran who fought under Eisenhower or a college student who was not even born at the time, believes that if Eisenhower had taken the city the Americans would have full possession of it today.

There is no basis for such a belief. If Eisenhower's armies had captured Berlin, they would have withdrawn beyond the Elbe River in July, with the Russians taking over their zone, plus their sector of Berlin. After that, events would have transpired as they in fact did. The Berlin Blockade would still have taken place; the Berlin Wall would still be there.

A second myth is that Eisenhower received orders from

President Franklin D. Roosevelt to leave Berlin to the Russians. The story is that Roosevelt made a deal with Stalin at Yalta—in some extreme versions because the President was a traitor, in more popular ones because he was a sick man who did not know what he was doing. It is at least possible to trace the origins of this myth.

On April 22, 1945, Drew Pearson wrote in the *Washington Post:* "Though it may get official denial the real fact is that American advance patrols on Friday, April 13, one day after President Roosevelt's death, were in Potsdam, which is to Berlin what the Bronx is to New York City . . . [but] the next day withdrew from the Berlin suburbs to the River Elbe about 50 miles south. This withdrawal was ordered largely because of a previous agreement with the Russians that they were to occupy Berlin and because of their insistence that the agreement be kept."

Vehement denials by those who had been at Yalta with Roosevelt—led by Harry Hopkins—did no good, nor has it helped to point out that no Americans ever got near Potsdam. The myth that Roosevelt made a deal with Stalin was firmly implanted. It will probably never be rooted out. For the record, neither of the two presidents under whom Eisenhower served during World War II ever interfered with his operations in the slightest. General Eisenhower alone made the decision to stop at the Elbe.

Because of all the mythology surrounding the problem, some of the arguments in this essay are based on speculation. This is poor history, but it seems to me that in the case of Berlin it is necessary. I make no claim to uncovering new material; essentially we have known for years what happened and what the participants said to each other. Despite this knowledge, the discussion of the Berlin decision seems to be stuck in a rut. It may be that speculation is the only way to get it out. Further documentation on the motives of the governmental leaders is needed; when it becomes available it will clarify the problem. All quotations and statements of fact in this essay have previously appeared in print.

I do not here present a definitive statement on the Berlin decision. Rather I have tried to describe the military situation and then raise questions and make suggestions. Berlin in 1945 marked both the end of the great wartime alliance and the beginning of the Cold War. It is a subject that deserves the most intensive study. If this essay serves to stimulate a continuation of the debate over the Berlin decision, it will serve a purpose; I hope that it can carry the debate forward.

Because my own prejudices have affected my thinking, they should be stated. Fundamentally I admire President Roosevelt's political strategy, which was one of trying to continue the alliance beyond the defeat of the enemy. The best hope for the world in 1945 was American-Russian co-operation, and the achievement of this aim was worth almost any effort. I do not believe that the hope was doomed from the start.

For the past three years I have worked daily with the papers of General Eisenhower. I therefore tend to see every problem of World War II from his point of view. I sympathize with his approach to the problems and nearly always agree with his solutions. One of the readers of this essay says it is a "brief for the defense." Perhaps so. I can only say that each time I study the decision my feeling that Eisenhower's and Roosevelt's actions were both logical and correct is strengthened.

I have been blessed with uncommonly generous aid in the development of this essay. Professor Harold Hyman of the University of Illinois, General Editor of the Norton Essays in American History; Dr. Kent Roberts Greenfield of Baltimore; Dr. Forrest C. Pogue of the George C. Marshall Research Foundation; and Dr. Alfred D. Chandler, Jr., of the Johns Hoppins University all read the manuscript. Their advice and criticisms were invaluable. Mr. Edwin Alan Thompson, Research Associate of the Eisenhower Papers, provided me with many of the raw materials with which to work. Mrs. Elizabeth Smith, my typist, did her usual superb job.

My late wife did some of the research, typed all the notes, and was as always my first and most critical reader. Her role in the preparation of this essay, in fact, entitled her to a place on the title page. Her name does not appear there because of her diffidence and my pride.

Eisenhower and Berlin, 1945

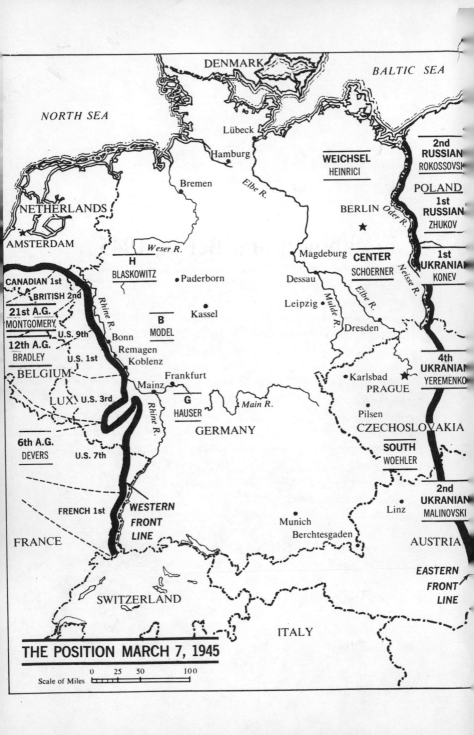

THE POSITION MARCH 7, 1945

1

The Position, March 7, 1945

~~~~~~

OF ALL THE FACTORS that influenced General Dwight D. Eisenhower's decision to stop at the Elbe River, few were more important than one brought about on March 7 by accident. At the beginning of the month Eisenhower had his armies either up to or closing on the line of the Rhine and Moselle rivers. The position represented a triumph for Eisenhower's strategy, for he had always hoped to fight a major battle with the Germans west of the Rhine River, thereby depleting their forces and making the crossing of the river and subsequent operations easier. Thanks in large part to Hitler's determination to fight for every inch of ground, Eisenhower was successful. After the battles west of the Rhine, the German armies left to defend the river were in an extremely weak condition. In addition, Eisenhower had finally attained an easily held defensive line, and could now afford to concentrate his strength for two or three crossings without worrying about a German counterattack.

As Supreme Commander, Allied Expeditionary Force, Eisenhower commanded a force of eight armies (one of which was in France and not at the front), organized into three army groups. The 21st Army Group to the north included the Canadian First Army, the British Second, and the American Ninth. The 12th Army Group in the center contained the American First and Third Armies. To the south, the 6th Army Group included the American Seventh and the French First Army. At the beginning of March, the Germans had seven armies organized into three army groups protecting the Rhine. The men

17

varied in quality from newly formed, untrained, and half-armed *Volkssturm* divisions to superb SS formations. The total number of soldiers the Germans had on the front may have equalled Eisenhower's total, but only a very small percentage of the German troops were first-class fighting men. In addition the Anglo-Americans had complete domination of the air. Whenever the weather was half-way decent, the Allied air forces made it impossible for the Germans to move along roads or railroads. The Germans had other problems; even when the weather kept the Allied planes out of the sky, the Germans did not have enough fuel to move their divisions around. They were low on ammunition, food, armor, medical supplies, and nearly everything else. They were capable of putting up a fight along a static front, but once the allied forces broke through the crust and the battle became mobile there was little if anything the Germans could do.

Eisenhower's plans were to make the major crossing in the north with Field Marshal Bernard L. Montgomery's 21st Army Group, with a secondary effort in the south, spearheaded by General George Patton's Third Army and directed through Frankfurt. The northern and southern forces would join hands well to the east of the Rhine, thus encircling the Ruhr River area, with its heavy industry, and cutting off the German armies there. After the link-up they would turn east and overrun the rest of Germany, presumably with 21st Army Group (the only army group that contained three armies) leading the way along the north coast and on into Berlin. The southern forces in General Omar Bradley's 12th Army Group would play a supporting role.

Then, on March 7, as elements of General Courtney Hodges' American First Army were clearing the west bank of the Rhine, members of the 9th Armored Division found the Ludendorff Bridge at Remagen intact. They rushed across and seized the opposite bank just in time to prevent the Germans from blowing the bridge. The news quickly moved up the chain of command, reaching Bradley that evening. Bradley was talking to Eisenhower's G-3, General Harold R. ("Pinky") Bull, about a

SHAEF (Supreme Headquarters, Allied Expeditionary Force) proposal to shift four divisions from 12th Army Group to 6th Army Group in the south. Bradley was furious. He told Bull the proposal was "larcenous." Bull shouted back, "By gosh, but you people are difficult to get along with, and I might add that you are getting more difficult every day."

"But SHAEF has had experience," Bradley replied, "in getting along with difficult people." Bull glared, then snapped, "The 12th Army Group is no harder to get along with than 21st Group. But you can take it from me, it's no easier either." [1]

At that point Hodges called to tell Bradley of the capture of the Ludendorff Bridge. "Hot dog, Courtney," Bradley said, and told him to get as much stuff over the river as he could.

After hanging up, Bradley turned on Bull, grinned, thumped him on the back, and laughed. "There goes your ball game, Pink. Courtney's gotten across the Rhine on a bridge." Bull shrugged and said that did not make any difference, because nobody was going anywhere at Remagen. "It just doesn't fit into *the* plan."

"Plan—hell," Bradley retorted, and called Eisenhower. The Supreme Commander was delighted. "Hold on to it, Brad," he said. "Get across with whatever you need—but make certain you hold that bridgehead." [2]

It was a crucial decision. Under the existing plan Montgomery was to get the bulk of the available supplies and equipment; after his needs were satisfied, Bradley could have what remained. By committing his forces across the Rhine, Bradley would be in a position to make priority claims on supplies. Bull recognized this immediately, and accused Bradley of seeking to force Eisenhower to make a diversion of forces from Montgomery. "Ike's heart is in your sector," Bull explained, "but right now his mind is up north." [3]

1. Omar N. Bradley, *A Soldier's Story* (New York, 1951), 517.
2. *Ibid.*, 510–11; Dwight D. Eisenhower, *Crusade in Europe* (New York, 1948), 380; Chester Wilmot, *The Struggle for Europe* (London, 1952), 675.
3. Bradley, *A Soldier's Story*, 512–13.

Bull's assumption that Eisenhower's plan was rigid was mistaken. Eisenhower's outstanding tactical characteristic was flexibility. He never allowed his mind to become set or rigid, and he was usually successful in creating tactical situations that presented him with a number of alternatives. This allowed him to exploit any lucky break. He was well aware that his greatest strength was in the north with 21st Army Group, and he knew even better than Montgomery that an advance north of the Ruhr was the quickest way to deny the Germans access to their industries there. Eisenhower agreed with Montgomery that the Westphalian plains on the road to Berlin offered excellent terrain for mobile warfare. But he also knew that there were other routes into central Germany and that the imperative requirement was speed. However it was done, Eisenhower wanted to end the war as soon as possible. He had the Germans on the run and in those circumstances any idea of pausing to regroup was anathema to him. He would give his total support to any commander who promised to keep the Germans running. The man who would do that best, Eisenhower felt, was Bradley.

Bradley and Montgomery had been arguing ever since the breakout at Normandy over the proper strategy for the campaign. Both tried to "get to" Eisenhower and swing him to their point of view, and both went through frequent periods of extreme bitterness when they felt Eisenhower had favored the other. In general terms, Montgomery advocated a single thrust into Germany carried out by his 21st Army Group, while Bradley wanted a broad front advance. Both were unhappy with what they considered Eisenhower's wavering. For example, following a meeting in late August, 1944, Bradley felt that the Supreme Commander had opted for the single thrust and that "Monty had won the initial skirmish." [4] Montgomery felt that his arguments were "to no avail" and that the broad front strategy had been adopted.[5]

4. *Ibid.,* 400.
5. Bernard Law Montgomery, *The Memoirs of Field-Marshal the Viscount Montgomery of Alamein, K. G.* (Cleveland, 1958), 241.

The chief difference between Bradley and Montgomery in their relationships with Eisenhower was that Bradley respected his chief's tactical and strategical abilities while Montgomery was contemptuous of them. Montgomery's closest friend was the Chief of the Imperial General Staff, Field Marshal Alan Brooke. The two British officers shared the same view of Eisenhower. Brooke dotted his diary with comments of this sort: "It is clear that Ike knows nothing about strategy." [6] Before the invasion, Brooke had analyzed Eisenhower as "a past-master in the handling of allies, entirely impartial and consequently trusted by all. A charming personality and good co-ordinator. But no real commander." Eisenhower, Brooke declared, was "just a co-ordinator, a good mixer, a champion of inter-Allied co-operation." [7]

Both Brooke and Montgomery misjudged Eisenhower. They thought that his basic honesty and modesty indicated a sense of professional inferiority in planning campaigns and handling operations. They saw Eisenhower as a man reluctant to make a decision and dangerously open to persuasion by the last strong man to whom he talked. Consequently they—especially Montgomery—felt it was necessary to bombard the Supreme Commander with their views, so that those views would always be before him.[8] In fact Eisenhower's plans, although they may have been wrong, were well thought out, and throughout the war he resisted Brooke's and Montgomery's very strenuous, often irritating, and always untactful efforts to get him to change. Still they persisted, to the point that by 1945 Eisenhower was disgusted with Montgomery.

The senior British officers at Eisenhower's headquarters shared their commander's feelings. Eisenhower's Deputy, Air Chief Marshal Arthur Tedder, had on at least one occasion urged Montgomery's relief. The Deputy Operations Chief, Gen-

6. Arthur Bryant, *Triumph in the West* (New York, 1959), 181.
7. *Ibid.,* 139.
8. Wilmot, *Struggle for Europe,* 467–68, who agrees with Brooke and Montgomery, gives the best expression of this attitude towards Eisenhower.

eral John Whiteley, recalled after the war that "Monty wanted to ride into Berlin on a white charger wearing two hats, but the feeling was that if anything was to be done quickly, don't give it to Monty." The British Deputy Chief of Staff declared, "At that moment Monty was the last person Ike would have chosen for a drive on Berlin—Monty would have needed at least six months to prepare." [9]

Eisenhower's personal feelings toward Montgomery were unusual. The Supreme Commander was a gregarious man, who fitted into any situation because he attuned to others perfectly, mixing easily with individuals who varied in personality from the high-strung, bombastic Patton to the emotionally stable, low-keyed Bradley. He was able to adjust himself so that he could talk frankly, directly, and most of all effectively to such disparate types as Charles de Gaulle, Winston Churchill, and Franklin Roosevelt. He had his temper under tight control, revealing his own anxieties only through his chain smoking. Seldom in four years, during which time he had to deal with countless megalomaniacs, innumerable irritating problems, and dozens of major crises, did he lose his temper. He did not carry over into the next day the problems of the moment; he approached every decision on its own merits. He could do so because he liked people and therefore enjoyed life. A few minutes in the evening playing bridge or poker refreshed him.

Eisenhower was ideal as an allied commander because of his intense desire to have everybody get along with everybody else. He felt strongly about things and on occasion was forced to insist upon his own solution—he was perhaps the only man who ever submitted to a six-hour barrage from Churchill and, although failing to convince the Prime Minister, emerged with his own views unchanged. But when confronted with a problem, Eisenhower's instinctive reaction was to seek a solution that everyone could live with, perhaps a reflection of his having grown up in a small house filled with younger and older broth-

9. Cornelius Ryan, *The Last Battle* (New York, 1966), 241.

ers. Whereas Montgomery, and to an extent Bradley, was inclined to hold out for the whole show, to demand his conception of the ideal solution, Eisenhower tended to be a compromiser, if a compromise could be found.

But he was not a waverer. He stuck so closely to his original conception for operations in Europe that after the war he could justly claim that few campaigns in history had developed in as close accord with their plans. In simplest terms, he had aimed to overrun France, bring his forces up to the Rhine River, make at least two and possibly three crossings, encircle the Ruhr, and then spread through Germany. Montgomery and Brooke wanted to dash on to Berlin across the northern route, with absolute priority in supplies going to the 21st Army Group. Eisenhower could never agree to limit his forces to that one approach to Germany. By keeping his right wing up with or close to the left, he forced the Germans to disperse their forces to meet the double threat. The broad front approach made it possible for Eisenhower to employ more troops in the offensive, and the United States had been bulging with troops trained to fight and ready to come to Europe. If Eisenhower had chosen the single thrust, most of these men could not have been used. The broad front allowed SHAEF to draw on more roads and thereby support more troops. Those advancing on the right linked up with the forces coming up through southern France (Operation AN-VIL) and therefore could draw on the port capacity of Marseille. They cut off some 200,000 German troops remaining behind the point of the junction and thus eliminated them from the war.[10]

10. Eisenhower, *Crusade in Europe*, 255–59. "Looking back over the eleven months of fighting which were required to defeat the German armies," Eisenhower's Chief of Staff later declared, "I can say very sincerely that I do not believe a great campaign has ever been fought before with so little change in its original strategic plan. The grand strategy for OVERLORD which was agreed upon at SHAEF before the troops were ever put aboard ship for the invasion was followed almost without alteration. Tactical changes were made as the German reaction called for them, but the strategic plan was not changed." Walter Bedell Smith, *Eisenhower's Six Great Decisions* (New York, 1956), 211.

The British were well aware that Eisenhower's strategy resulted in a final triumph. The trouble was, they felt, that it took too long. After the war, charges about Eisenhower's lack of boldness became very popular in Great Britain. One reason for this was that the British, following a great victory in the greatest war in their history, needed some explanation for British weakness in the postwar world. The explanation often proposed was that the last six months of the war proved too much of a drain on British manpower and industrial capacity. If the war had ended before Christmas, 1944, Britain could have recovered from victory and continued to play the role of a great power. But the British convinced themselves that this quick victory, essential to their war-weary economy, was lost because of Eisenhower's strategy.

Montgomery, although far from alone in making the claim, has presented it best. In his memoirs he contends that he saw in the summer of 1944 that the British economy and manpower situation demanded victory before Christmas. "Our 'must,' " he declares, was "different from the American must; a difference in urgency." The Americans did not understand this, they were afraid to take risks, and they were willing to wait for a sure conclusion rather than gamble on a quick one.[11]

It is true that Eisenhower's *tactical* tendency was toward caution. He had to be certain of a conclusive victory, if only because, with the superiority of men and equipment the British and American people had provided him, there was no excuse for his losing. Within the context of that requirement, Eisenhower did take calculated risks. It is true that in directing operations Eisenhower, notwithstanding the abundance of resources that the British and American peoples had put at his disposal, avoided staking his superiority on a single *tactical* throw. But with regard to the readiness of Eisenhower and the Americans

11. Montgomery, *Memoirs*, 243. Montgomery believes that Eisenhower was unwilling to risk a defeat in the fall of 1944 because of the upcoming Presidential elections. There is absolutely no evidence to support such a charge.

to take *strategic* risks in order to end the war sooner, Montgomery's criticism ignored Eisenhower's leading role in 1942 in urging a cross-Channel invasion that fall, if necessary, with an all-out invasion not later than 1943, when the British were unwilling to do more than campaign in the Mediterranean.

Montgomery was commanding troops from a nation that had already made tremendous sacrifices, and he felt that the British would be hurt more than the Germans by a campaign of attrition. Eisenhower and Bradley came from a society and a tradition that always promised and usually provided overwhelming superiority everywhere. The American doctrine was to use that superiority to hit the enemy all along the front all the time. The Americans had not fully mobilized, could well afford losses, and were more than willing to stand up and trade blows with the Germans.[12]

By March, 1945, it was too late for the British to change the general conception of the campaign. Eisenhower had insisted on the broad front approach, had won his victory west of the Rhine, and had his troops drawn up along the river. It was not too late, however, for the British to make one last attempt to have Eisenhower concentrate everything in the north and make a dash for Berlin.

There were many reasons involved in the British advocacy of such a strategy, not least of which was national prestige. By this time the Americans had nearly twelve million men in arms, the British only five million. The Americans were dictating strategy throughout the world, a practice that was galling to the Chief of the Imperial General Staff. He also felt it was dangerous, since he considered the Americans to be neophytes in the field. But all Brooke could do about it was to commit bitter comments to his diary or send cutting remarks about the Americans to Montgomery. He did a good deal of both.[13] Other Englishmen felt the same way. As early as January, 1944, Churchill was pro-

12. Wilmot, *Struggle for Europe*, 338–40, has a good discussion of this point.
13. See Bryant, *Triumph in the West*, 167–68.

pounding strategies "based on ensuring that British troops were retained in the limelight, if necessary, at the expense of the Americans." [14] The reaction was understandable. The British had, after all, stemmed the Nazi tide. Had the island race crumbled in 1940 or 1941, Hitler almost certainly would have been the master of all of Europe, Russia, North Africa and the Near East. Now, in 1945, the Russians and Americans had emerged as the twin powers of the world, incomparably stronger than any other nation. They were getting too much of the credit for the defeat of Germany. It seemed only fair that the British play a leading role in the last scene of the last act—that, in short, the British be allowed to dominate the climactic finale, the capture of Berlin.

This, the British felt, could be done easily enough if Eisenhower would agree to give SHAEF's full support to 21st Army Group and direct it toward Berlin. Specifically, aside from granting Montgomery priority in supplies, Eisenhower would have to give 21st Army Group the use of the American Ninth Army. Otherwise Montgomery would not be strong enough to break through to Berlin, for without American support he had only two armies under his command, the British Second and the Canadian First. The key question, then, became not so much one of directives as of administration: under whom would Ninth Army fight, Montgomery or Bradley? If it fought with 21st Army Group, the big push would be in the north.

Throughout the war Eisenhower had tried to refrain from making any decision on nationalistic grounds. He wished always to direct his operations in response to only one criterion— sound military practice. It was an extremely difficult task, one that no previous commander of an alliance had accomplished. Even Eisenhower, the most successful alliance commander in history, had sometimes to bow to national pressures, as when, during the Battle of the Bulge, Charles de Gaulle was able to persuade him to hold Strasbourg for political reasons when Eisenhower wanted to pull back and shorten his line for military

14. *Ibid.*, 282.

reasons. The British complained that most of Eisenhower's operations were dictated by politics, that he adhered to a broad front strategy only because he would otherwise have to stop Patton to supply Montgomery and that this was something that as an American he just would not do. They were mistaken. Eisenhower's concept may have been wrong, but it was based solely on military grounds as he saw them.[15]

Eisenhower was not overly concerned with the problem of which nation deserved the prestige of striking the final blow. He saw his task as one of finishing the war as quickly as possible, and unless instructed otherwise he would conduct his operations with that one end in view. The British would, during the next month, advance innumerable arguments designed to force Eisenhower to turn his full attention to Berlin, but he refused to listen to any of them. His orders from his superiors, the Combined Chiefs of Staff, were clear, and he was determined to adhere to them. In their directive to Eisenhower for the campaign, the

15. Patton felt that Eisenhower went too far in his efforts to avoid nationalism, and used to mutter that "Ike is the best damn general the British have got." Two stories by Lord Ismay illustrate Eisenhower's approach to alliance command. Very early in the war, when Americans were just building up their forces in England, Ismay heard of an American officer who when drinking would boast that his troops would show the British how to fight. Ismay brought the matter to Eisenhower's attention. Eisenhower "went white with rage." He summoned an aide and told him to arrange for the officer in question to report the next morning. As the aide left the room, Eisenhower hissed to Ismay, "I'll make the son of a bitch swim back to America." Ismay said that if he had known Eisenhower was going to take such an extreme view he would never have brought up the matter. Eisenhower turned his wrath on Ismay. "If we are not going to be frank with each other, however delicate the topic," Eisenhower declared, "we will never win this war." Sometime later, Eisenhower learned of a fracas between an American and a British officer on his staff. He investigated, decided that the American was at fault, ordered him reduced in rank, and sent back to the States. The British officer protested. "He only called me the son-of-a-bitch, sir, and all of us have now learnt that this is a colloquial expression which is sometimes used almost as a term of endearment." To which Eisenhower replied, "I am informed that he called you a British son-of-a-bitch. That is quite different. My ruling stands." Hastings L. Ismay, *The Memoirs of General Lord Ismay* (New York, 1960), 258–59, 263.

Combined Chiefs of Staff ordered him to "enter the continent of Europe, and, in conjunction with the other United Nations [Russia], undertake operations aimed at the heart of Germany and the destruction of her armed forces." [16] At a critical point in the campaign, Eisenhower told the Combined Chiefs of Staff that if they wished for him to try for Berlin for political reasons, they had only to order him to do so and he would cheerfully obey. Until then, however, he intended to run a purely military campaign. The Combined Chiefs of Staff did not change his directive.

Eisenhower's attitude was consistent both with American tradition and his own previous conduct. In the United States, the separation of the civilian from the military, together with the idea that the military carry out orders from civilian superiors and do not engage in any way in politics, is a deeply ingrained principle. The American soldier who engages in politics while in uniform is so exceptional that he probably shocks his fellow officers more than he frightens civilians. This applies both to domestic politics and foreign policy. It is, perhaps, an unsophisticated position, since it is easy enough to demonstrate that in fact any military decision has political consequences. Soldiers are as aware of this as are the social scientists, although they often write as if they can make clear distinctions between political and military factors (this is especially true of the generals involved in the Berlin decision who wrote their memoirs). They like to feel that they are responding to clear-cut orders, that they are only carrying out policy decided by higher authority. In fact, however, the situation is always much more complicated than that. What the soldiers do try and accomplish —and in the Berlin case they were successful—is to make sure their actions are in accord with national policy. As implementers of that policy, they make countless political decisions,

---

16. Forrest C. Pogue, *The Supreme Command* (in Kent Roberts Greenfield, ed. *United States Army in World War II*) (Washington, 1954), 53. The full directive is reprinted as Appendix B to the present essay.

but not the basic ones. In March and April, 1945, any attempt on the part of the Western armies to capture Berlin before the Russians got there would have had enormous political overtones. The possible results of such a move were clear enough to everyone involved. A decision to make the attempt would have marked a fundamental change in current American foreign policy (which was geared to the hope that the wartime alliance could be continued into the postwar world). Eisenhower felt that he was not the man to make such a decision.

There is much confusion over terminology on political-military relationships, because there is no sharp line separating a "military decision" from a "political decision." Quoting Clausewitz's famous dictum is not enough to clarify the point. Eisenhower's decision to defeat Germany as fast as possible, while seemingly a straightforward military decision, was in fact rooted in political considerations—this was what the American and British people wanted. His desire to avoid conflict with the Russians at all costs was an extension of the basic political strategy of the entire war.

Eisenhower's commander in chief had repeatedly made the basic position clear—President Roosevelt wanted to defeat Germany and eliminate the Nazi threat to world civilization, and he wanted to continue the working partnership with the Russians after the war. If the United States and the Soviet Union did not co-operate, he felt, there would be no real peace, and the sacrifices of the war would have been in vain. Roosevelt would go to great lengths to maintain the alliance; in April, 1945, the Russians grew indignant over the manner in which the West handled the surrender of the German forces in Italy. Stalin felt he was being duped and accused Churchill and Roosevelt of duplicity. The Prime Minister was highly insulted and wanted the President to join him in the strongest possible protest to Stalin. Roosevelt, however, in one of his last messages, declared, "I would minimize the general Soviet problem as much as possible, because these problems, in one form or another, seem to arise every day, and most of them straighten out . . ." [17]

There can be legitimate debate about the wisdom of the President's policy. There can be no doubt, however, as to what his policy was; it is equally clear that Eisenhower was trying to act within the context of the wishes of his political superior. The general felt strongly that it was neither his right nor his responsibility to question or change the President's policy.

Whether Eisenhower was right or wrong in his refusal to make fundamental political decisions, no one could have been surprised at his basic position, for it was the one upon which he had stood throughout the war. In 1944, for example, after the successful landings at Normandy, Churchill had raised the question of further operations in the Mediterranean. Eisenhower wanted a landing in the south of France; Churchill wanted to push operations in Italy or else land in the Adriatic and pursue an offensive through what he liked to refer to as the "soft underbelly" of Europe. The climax of the argument came with a six-hour conference between Churchill and Eisenhower. The Prime Minister used all of his considerable oratorical talents to try and persuade Eisenhower to his point of view. Eisenhower continued to say no. Time and again during the long afternoon, Eisenhower said that if Churchill had political reasons for wanting to abandon the south of France landings in favor of operations in the Balkans, the Prime Minister should go to the President with them. If Roosevelt agreed that for political reasons the campaign should be undertaken, Eisenhower would of course change his plans.

Even in this case, there was no sharp separation of political and military considerations. What Eisenhower was saying, in part, was that if Churchill wished to change the political objective of the war he would have to go to the President to do so. Eisenhower knew that America's political objective was the defeat of Germany; he was not going to change that objective because the head of a foreign government, albeit an allied one,

17. Winston S. Churchill, *Triumph and Tragedy* (*The Second World War,* Vol. VI) (Boston, 1953), 454.

wanted him to. If his superiors decided that forestalling the Russians in central Europe was more important than eliminating the German threat, Eisenhower would modify his military plans. Churchill, however, consistently replied that politics had nothing to do with it. He said the course of action he advocated was the militarily correct one. Eisenhower said that it was not, and on military grounds he would refuse to consider the change.[18]

For Eisenhower the problem in early March, 1945, was how to defeat the Germans as soon as possible. In part the question had already been answered by his decision to reinforce the bridgehead at Remagen—the main pursuit east of the Rhine would go into central, not northern, Germany. But the action at Remagen was not irrevocable. The bridgehead could be used only as a threat, forcing the Germans to shift troops from the north in an attempt to contain it and thus giving Montgomery more freedom of action. Eisenhower could still make his main push in the north, leaving Ninth Army to Montgomery and engaging the Russians in a race to Berlin. In short, Eisenhower still had alternatives.

The question of how most quickly to defeat the Germans refined itself down to the question of who would exploit better, Bradley or Montgomery? For Eisenhower, as for his staff at SHAEF (which at the higher levels was more British than American), the answer was obvious: Bradley. This was both a considered judgment and an emotional reaction. Eisenhower was temperamentally close to his fellow American. They were classmates at West Point, shared the same traditions, and talked the same language. One of the biggest problems Eisenhower had with Montgomery throughout the campaign was simple misunderstanding, something which seldom occurred in his relationship with Bradley. Above all, Eisenhower felt that Bradley had the drive, energy, and ability to exploit the victory that had been won west of the Rhine. He appreciated Montgomery's many

18. Eisenhower, *Crusade in Europe,* 284.

outstanding qualities as a soldier, but doubted that they included those required for an exploitation.

There were other factors in the situation. Eisenhower and Bradley shared strategical concepts that were antithetical to those of Montgomery. Montgomery was deeply steeped in the British tradition, a tradition of fighting with inferior forces against continental powers. He believed in forcing the enemy to commit his reserves on a wide front, then committing his own reserves on a narrow front in a hard blow. He was cautious—to a fault, it seemed to the Americans—and never struck his blow until he was assured of victory. Some Americans felt that he was so blown up over his reputation gained at El Alamein that he would never, under any circumstances, risk a defeat. In view of his operations at Arnhem in the Fall of 1944 this was an unfair charge. Still, he did believe implicitly in the doctrine of concentration at the vital point, and he hesitated to move until he had overwhelming superiority at that point. During the Normandy battle, Eisenhower and his staff were concerned over the slowness of Montgomery's movements, and at that time there was talk at SHAEF of sacking him. Even Churchill joined in the chorus of complaints.[19] Montgomery's caution showed again after the breakout, when his failure to push his troops allowed the Germans to escape from the Falaise trap. During the race through France, Bradley's 12th Army Group, led by Patton's Third Army, was spectacularly more successful in the pursuit than 21st Army Group. Even allowing for the obvious fact that Montgomery always faced stronger opposition than did the Americans, his several abilities did not seem to extend to a pell-mell exploitation.

Pursuit had an enormous appeal to the Americans, both because of the American command system and the American personality. In the American army, unlike the British, corps and division commanders had the widest possible latitude. They used it to push ahead in a blitzkrieg that left the Germans gasping. Soldiers and officers alike were undaunted by distance. A

19. Bryant, *Triumph in the West,* 170–79.

mechanically oriented people, Americans were accustomed to long automobile drives, even as ordinary pleasure outings on Sunday afternoons. Nearly every soldier in 12th Army Group had known how to drive an automobile since he was sixteen years old. Many of them had taken apart and put back together an engine; it was a rare company that did not include at least one private who was an expert on the workings of the internal combustion engine. American armored and motorized divisions could make their own repairs on the road and keep pushing forward. No other nation could send into the field troops that could match the Americans in these attributes. Bradley's armies could exploit a victory better than any other soldiers in the world's history.

The British simply could not psychologically convert their infantry into motorized divisions, even when trucks were available, because by nature the commanders and the men moved at a deliberate pace. In Bradley's command every infantry division, not to mention armored, was capable of swift and bold exploitation. In Montgomery's command even the armored divisions were stodgy by comparison.[20]

These differences became even clearer when the armies reached the Rhine. Montgomery's preparations for the crossing were so careful, the superiority he insisted upon gaining over the Germans before beginning so great, that it became a joke among the Americans. Eisenhower's comment was the most polite: "Montgomery was always a master in the methodical preparation of forces for a formal, set-piece attack. In this case he made the most meticulous preparations because we knew that along the front just north of the Ruhr the enemy had his best remaining troops." [21] By contrast, Bradley had pushed across at the first opportunity, and Patton was ready to take the Rhine "on the run," crossing as soon as he got there. "Bradley," Eisenhower once told an aide, "has never held back and never

20. Wilmot makes this point with great insight. *Struggle for Europe,* 427.
21. Eisenhower, *Crusade in Europe,* 387.

has 'paused to re-group' when he saw an opportunity to advance." [22]

The lucky break at Remagen gave Eisenhower an opportunity to use Bradley's talents. His determination to exploit the crossing affected the plan for the German campaign and, in this sense, was the point of departure for the decision not to concentrate on a drive to Berlin. Eisenhower's reaction to the event illustrated the strategy with which he brought the war to a victorious conclusion for the Western allies—a strategy that did not change, from first to last, in its principles. The object was to win the war as quickly as possible. It was characterized by flexibility in exploiting options that Eisenhower kept open by advancing on a broad front. His application of it showed his preference for American commanders in the conduct of crucial operations. Montgomery's views and behavior, on the other hand, while partly personal, reflected the military traditions of the British. They also represented the position of the British in early 1945, when they felt the need for a resounding blow quickly achieved which would save British prestige and influence. Under different circumstances Eisenhower had shown himself willing to give the British such an opportunity, but at this late date he doubted Montgomery's ability to take real advantage of the opportunity.

When Eisenhower went to bed on the night of March 7, his mind was fixed on the single purpose of bringing the war to an early end. The situation was still fluid, his plans still flexible. But increasingly he was convinced that Bradley was the man who could do the job best.

22. Wilmot, *Struggle for Europe,* 691.

2

The Creation
of the Zones

ONE OF THE most important factors upon which Eisenhower
had to brood as he made his plans for the final offensive was the
absence of any agreed-upon meeting place with the Russians.
Each side was free to move as far forward as it could. This created a dangerous and worrisome, even a frightening situation
for the Supreme Commander, for he did not want his troops
getting involved through mistake in a bloody fire-fight with the
Red Army. As the American and British troops moved east and
the Russians west through Germany, some kind of clear
geographical feature would have to be found where they could
meet and stop.

The already settled zones of occupation for Germany were
of no help, for except in one or two spots they did not follow
geographical lines. Furthermore, the zones would only come
into operation following Germany's unconditional surrender;
they would play no role in the development of operations, and
no one proposed that they be used as stop lines. The zones, in
short, represented political, not military or geographic, lines.

The story of American participation in the creation of the
zones is a comedy of errors brought on by the incredibly poor
organization of President Roosevelt's wartime government. No
agency existed to co-ordinate the activities of the War Department and the State Department. Staff work was carried out by
men who had no responsibility for operations, and operations
were carried out by men who had no chance to participate in

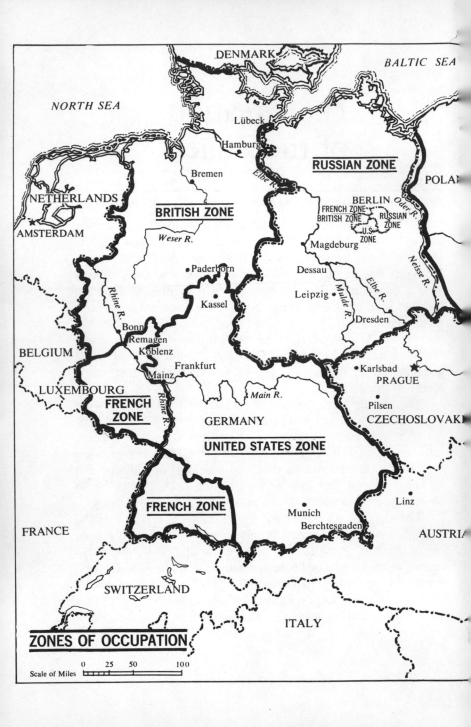

ZONES OF OCCUPATION

the planning process.[1] Only one man was in a position to hold the strings together, and he was by this time old, forgetful, and dying. From the beginning of the war Roosevelt was determined to act as his own defense committee. Shortly after Pearl Harbor, Secretary of State Cordell Hull had suggested that he, Hull, should participate in the President's discussions with the War Department, "particularly on those [matters] of a combined military and diplomatic nature." Hull, maintaining that all important military decisions had political overtones, said he might contribute to the discussions, and asked that at any rate he be kept informed of developments. But although the active participation of the foreign minister in the higher war councils was a commonplace in Great Britain and Russia, the President said no.[2] The result of Roosevelt's attitude was that when the time came to draw up plans for the postwar treatment of Germany the State Department was not involved, while the War Department, which was, had no political guidance other than some vaguely expressed wishes from the President.

The first planning was done in 1943 by a combined agency, COSSAC (Chief of Staff to the Supreme Allied Commander, Designate), headed by the British General Sir Frederick Morgan. Morgan's chief task was to plan the invasion, Operation OVERLORD. In addition, however, the Combined Chiefs of Staff told him to prepare for a sudden collapse within Germany, such as subsequently might have occurred following the July 20, 1944, attempt on Hitler's life. Code name for this emergency operation was RANKIN; under it British troops would occupy northwestern Germany, the Russians would move into eastern Germany, and the Americans would take over the southern section. The lines Morgan drew to separate the three sections were

1. See John C. Ries, *The Management of Defense: Organization and Control of the U.S. Armed Services* (Baltimore, 1964), for a good discussion of staff and line functions in the War Department; see Arthur M. Schlesinger, Jr., *The Coming of the New Deal* (New York, 1959), for a defense of Roosevelt's administrative practices.
2. William M. Franklin, "Zonal Boundaries and Access to Berlin," *World Politics,* XVI (October, 1963), 1.

quite close to those finally adopted.[3]

When Roosevelt saw Morgan's plan he was upset. He did not see why Berlin and the surrounding area had to be assigned to the Russians, and he did not want American troops in southern Germany, because there the only way they could be supplied would be through French ports, and Roosevelt did not trust the French. Roosevelt's military advisers, led by Chief of Staff George Marshall, tried to explain to him that the British were in the northwest and the Americans in the south as a result of their respective positions in the proposed drive through France and into Germany, when the British would be on the left and the Americans on the right. This in turn resulted from the positions of the national forces in the initial landings on the Normandy beachhead, which in its turn resulted from the position of American troops stationed in England. The Americans had been stationed in southwestern England, the area of the island closest to the United States and thus most easily reached by convoys; this positioning put them on the right flank in the Normandy landings. To try and put the British on the right and the Americans on the left would have involved a cross-over in mid-Channel between the Americans coming from Dartmouth and Portland and the British steaming out of Portsmouth; since thousands of ships were involved, to attempt such a cross-over would have been, at best, hazardous, and in fact no one ever seriously considered it. Later, once ashore, to try and leap-frog, passing the British to the right and the Americans to the left, would have involved difficult, if not insurmountable, logistical problems. Roosevelt airily dismissed the problem, and on the American side nothing further was done.

Churchill, meanwhile, had created from his War Cabinet an Armistice and Post-War Committee, headed by Clement Attlee.

---

3. Frederick Morgan, *Overture to OVERLORD* (New York, 1950), 104–22. There had never been any question about occupation of Germany; the allies were determined to avoid the mistake, as they saw it, of 1918. How long occupying troops would remain in Germany was an open question; that they would be there was not.

Toward the end of the summer of 1943, the Attlee Committee submitted its report, which was essentially the final plan as it was worked out in 1945. The committee divided Germany into three national zones, with the boundaries those that were eventually accepted. Berlin would be jointly occupied. The Americans would have the southern zone, the British the northwestern, and the Russians the eastern. Churchill's War Cabinet approved the plan in the fall of 1943; for some reason Churchill did not submit it to the Americans at that time.[4]

Instead, the next step was a tripartite one, with the Big Three agreeing to create a European Advisory Commission to deal with the problems of postwar Germany. Membership of the European Advisory Commission consisted of John G. Winant, the American Ambassador to the United Kingdom, F. T. Gusev, the Russian Ambassador, and Sir William Strang of the British Foreign Office. The European Advisory Commission held its first formal session on January 14, 1944, in London. The next day Strang presented a draft instrument for German surrender which included a plan for the military occupation of Germany—the Attlee Committee report. A month later, Gusev presented the Soviet draft; the Russian proposal for zones of occupation was identical with the British proposal. Winant, who had received no instructions whatsoever, wired anxiously for guidance.

Washington was astonished that the British and Russians had reached such easy agreement. Roosevelt sent a note to the State Department: "What are the zones in the British and Russian drafts and what is the zone we are proposing? I must know this in order that it conform with what I decided on months ago." The President's memorandum baffled the State Department, since no one there had any idea of what he had "decided months ago." When Roosevelt learned this, he declared that whatever happened he would not have American troops in southern Germany, dependent upon the French for their lines of

4. Franklin, "Zonal Boundaries," *op. cit.,* 7–8; Winston S. Churchill, *Triumph and Tragedy,* 507–08.

communication. He did not want to get involved in the "post-war burden of reconstituting France, Italy and the Balkans," which he said "is definitely a British task." On February 29 he wired Churchill, "I denounce in protest the paternity of Belgium, France and Italy. You really ought to bring up and discipline your own children. In view of the fact that they may be your bulwark in future days, you should at least pay for the schooling now!"

The War Department, meanwhile, was disturbed because the State Department was getting involved. Army officers felt that the subject of zones was a military matter, which they had neither authority nor desire to discuss with State Department officials. The Army was willing to accept the southern zone; State followed the President's lead and insisted on the north-western. The effect of the disagreement was paralyzing; it was months before the American government could agree on instructions to send to its representative on the European Advisory Commission. Winant's position at European Advisory Commission meetings was increasingly embarrassing. Roosevelt reportedly had a good chuckle over the bickering.

The confusion, it must be emphasized, did not extend to the question of the western boundary of the Russian zone. This, and the joint occupation by all three powers of Berlin, was something the President, the War Department, and the State Department were all willing to accept. Earlier, in 1943, Roosevelt had indicated that he wanted Berlin for the Americans, and had even sketched on a map an American zone that extended from Stettin on the Baltic to the Czech border, thus putting Berlin and Leipzig in the American zone. At that time (November, 1943) he indicated he felt there "would definitely be a race for Berlin." Subsequently, however, he abandoned that idea, and after February, 1944, no one in the West seems to have advocated that either the British or the Americans take sole possession of Berlin. Since the Russians, who in human terms had made by far the greatest sacrifices in the war and contributed most to the defeat of Germany, were willing to settle for a joint occupation of the capital, Western statesmen were more than happy to agree. Roosevelt told the State Department to instruct Winant to accept the boundary separating the Russian from the Western zones, but to leave open the question of whether the Americans would be in the south or north.

At this time the Russians were still fighting on their own soil. In the north they had barely lifted the siege of Leningrad; in the center they were just up to the line of the Dnieper River; in the south they had pushed beyond the Dnieper but had not yet reached the Bug River and had so far failed to liberate the Crimea. The Western powers, meanwhile, were still four months away from the invasion of France. No one could tell whose forces would reach where, or even if an invasion of Germany itself would be necessary, since the Germans might quit first as they had done in 1918. The point is that the zones of occupation were *not* drawn up in accordance with projected military positions. They represented, rather, an attempt to divide Germany equally between the three powers. This is why the British and Russians came to such quick agreement—the Attlee Committee proposals represented a fairly equal division. It was only by chance that the onrushing armies did in fact meet near the center of Germany—it had never been planned that way. At various times it looked as if it would not happen; in September, 1944, for example, it appeared possible that Eisenhower's armies would overrun Germany in a few weeks and meet the Russians somewhere in Poland. In January, 1945, following the Battle of the Bulge and the Russian winter offensive, it seemed that the Russians might meet the Western armies along the banks of the Rhine River. Under the circumstances of a wildly fluctuating military situation, the governments could not, and wisely did not, draw up their postwar plans on the basis of military developments.

Most of what was going on at European Advisory Commission meetings was known to Eisenhower, and it displeased him. In January, 1944, before assuming his duties at SHAEF, he visited the United States and talked with Roosevelt in the White

House. Eisenhower objected to dividing Germany at all. He insisted that joint, as opposed to national, occupation of the entire country was desirable and practicable. If nothing else, Eisenhower said, it would "quickly test the possibilities" of continuing the war-time alliance. Roosevelt evidently gave the matter little thought, and no one else in authority seems to have considered it. Later Eisenhower advocated that after the war SHAEF remain intact and the Western powers at least carry out a joint occupation in their zones, but nothing came of that proposal either.

Although the boundary between the Anglo-American and Russian zones was fixed, British-American arguments over who should be in what zone continued throughout 1944. It became more complex when the question of a French zone entered the picture. Final agreement between the governments did not come until February, 1945; when it did, it was the Americans who gave in. The Americans took the southern zone and the Americans and British between them made room for a French zone. The Americans secured the right to use the port of Bremen to supply their troops, thus freeing them from dependence on the French, and got a written agreement from the British granting them transit rights across the British zone.[5] The joint occupation of Berlin and the western boundary of the Russian zone were accepted as originally proposed, over a year earlier.

The matter of access to Berlin has caused considerable furor by raising the question of why the Americans insisted upon written agreement on access rights to their southern zone when they did not insist upon written agreement on access rights to their Berlin sector. Partly the insistence reflected Roosevelt's attitude. He was convinced that he would receive more co-operation from the Russians than he would from the

5. This account is based primarily on Franklin, "Zonal Boundaries," *op. cit.* See also John Ehrman, *Grand Strategy: October 1944–August 1945* (J. R. M. Butler, ed., *History of the Second World War: United Kingdom Military Series,* Vol. VI) (London, 1956), 101–15; Ryan, *The Last Battle,* 149–54, 157–59, and the memoirs of the participants.

British. He delighted in saying that Stalin was "getatable" or in declaring that he could "handle Uncle Joe." As to the British, he once said that if the Americans took the southern zone "the British would undercut us in every move we make." [6] However mistaken he may have been in his attitude towards Stalin, Roosevelt's assumption and certainly his hope that co-operation between his country and the Soviet Union would carry over into the peace was, in the context of the times, inevitable. It was widely held in both the British and American governments, by the people, and by the press of the two countries. In any case the alternative, following the suffering of the past half-decade, was too grim to even think about.

More important, the European Advisory Commission agreement provided very specifically for the joint occupation of Berlin. The need for access from the West was obvious. Once the Soviets accepted Western presence in the city they also accepted the right of the West to get there. Indeed, some Westerners feared that if they raised the question of access rights they would call into question the right of the West to be in Berlin. Since the Soviets orally agreed that the right of the West to get to Berlin was implicit in the right of the West to be in the city at all, no one, including Roosevelt and Churchill, thought it wise to raise the subject of written guarantees with the Soviets. The American zone in southern Germany, on the other hand, was not an island in British-held territory, so there was no implicit right of access to it through the British zone. The Americans had alternative routes available; the British allowed them to come through the northwestern zone as a favor, not as a right. Thus this agreement had to be written. [7]

The European Advisory Commission made the final agreements on occupation zones in late 1944. Two questions remain: did the West ever propose to break the agreements, and did the existence of the zones affect military strategy? In both cases the answer is no.

6. Franklin, "Zonal Boundaries," *op. cit.*, 10.
7. *Ibid.*, 24–25.

In February, 1945, the Big Three met at Yalta, in the Crimea. It was a friendly meeting. Everyone was in a good mood because of the favorable military situation, and at no other conference of the war was agreement so easily reached. The Russians had just completed their winter offensive, one that carried them 300 miles forward and brought them to the line of the Oder and Neisse rivers, within thirty-five miles of Berlin. There they had paused to regroup and reform. The Red Army staff feared that the Germans, reacting to the threat to Berlin, would transfer their remaining divisions from the Western front in order to save the capital, and Stalin urged the British and Americans to attack with all possible speed and vigor. The West had a similar fear—that is, the British and Americans thought the Germans might recognize the Red Army's need to refit, and take advantage of it by transferring troops from the Eastern to the Western Front. Marshall and Brooke, therefore, urged the Red Army leaders to resume their offensive as soon as possible. No attempt was made to reach agreement on stop lines; destinations would be decided by the course of the battle, and where and how long the armies would remain after the war could be decided later by the heads of government.[8] Churchill, Roosevelt, Stalin, and their advisers were all concentrating on defeating Germany as fast as possible. They were not engaged in dark conspiracies to prevent the other side from capturing this or that place, all post-war myths to the contrary. As Churchill recorded, when the Soviet armies swarmed westward, "we wished them all success." By the same token, Stalin was anxious to see the West mount a huge offensive. "We separated in Crimea," Churchill later remembered, "as friends as well as Allies." [9]

8. Feis, *Churchill, Roosevelt, and Stalin* (Princeton, 1957), 498–99.
9. Churchill, *Triumph and Tragedy*, 510. A distinguished British historian has declared, "From a postwar point of view, the Americans were acting rightly when they insisted [in 1943] on driving into Germany, though of course this was not why they did it. If Stalin had been preparing for the cold war when he was still fighting the hot one, he would have urged the British and Americans to concentrate on southeast Europe [which was where Churchill wanted them to concentrate].

The most careful analysis of the situation is by John Ehrman. In the official British history of the war, he declares: "The British attitude at this stage should not be misunderstood. It is perhaps easy, in view of developments in the following decade, to see in it the emergence of a policy which later became orthodox throughout the Western world. But attitudes and policy should not be confused. In the first place, even if the Prime Minister and the Foreign Secretary . . . had decided in the spring of 1945 that action should be taken on the assumption that Russia might be a potential enemy, there was no likelihood of such action being adopted by their country or in the United States. But secondly, they did not so decide. Disappointed, distrustful and sometimes deeply alarmed as they were, their hopes, and British policy, rested on a continuing partnership of the three Powers expressed in and operating through the instrument of the United Nations . . ." [10]

Within this context, Churchill felt the best way to get along with the Russians was to deal with them from a position of strength. He thus became an advocate of shaking hands with the Soviets as far to the east as possible. He did feel that any parts of the Russian zone that Eisenhower's armies occupied should be held as bargaining points in a trading game with the Russians, but he never in any way advocated holding onto any part of the Russian zone permanently. [11]

They would have ended up with the Balkans, and Soviet forces would have been on the Rhine instead of on the Elbe. In fact, Stalin urged the Americans to attack Germany directly. This was the best strategy for war, but, from Stalin's point of view, the worst strategy for postwar." A. J. P. Taylor, *English History, 1914–1945* (New York and Oxford, 1965), 577.

10. John Ehrman, *Grand Strategy,* 150.

11. Churchill was most interested in food; the Russian zone contained the bulk of Germany's agricultural area, and he was leery of the drain on Great Britain if she had to feed the population of the British zone (a zone which included the Ruhr, Germany's richest industrial region). Churchill wanted Russian agreements to ship food into the British zone. Later, he may have thought he could use Western possession of Russian territory to get concessions on Poland, but this is doubtful. Like everyone else, he saw that nothing would get Stalin to back

Churchill's main interest in capturing Berlin was for reasons of prestige. The question his position raised was: prestige for what purpose? He declared in April that if the Russians captured both Berlin and Vienna their conviction that they had made the greatest contribution to victory would be strengthened. That conviction, however, was already so firmly implanted in the Russian mind—as a direct result of the loss of perhaps as many as 20 million Russians—that nothing could have shaken it. Neither Eisenhower nor his advisers were willing to sacrifice the lives of thousands of their men, risk at best a clash with the Russians and at worst the first battle of World War III, all for the sake of prestige, especially when they were convinced they could not get to the city first anyway, and even if they did would not be holding onto it.

More important was the conviction, at SHAEF and among the American armies, that any attempt to beat the Russians to Berlin would delay, not hasten, the end of the war. Eisenhower put the case most succinctly: "The future division of Germany did not influence our military plans for the final conquest of the country. Military plans, I believed, should be devised with the single aim of speeding victory; by later adjustment troops of the several nations could be concentrated into their own national sectors." [12]

His aim remained quick defeat, his purpose to overrun Germany, his method exploitation under his best general. One of his major problems remained the question of a stop line where his troops could meet the Russians without getting involved in any shooting. The agreements reached by the European Advisory Commission affected his plans and operations not at all, and had no bearing on his final decision to leave Berlin to the Russians.

---

down on that question. On the main point, Churchill told the President, "I am quite prepared to adhere to the occupational zones, but I do not wish our Allied troops or your American troops to be hustled back at any point by some crude assertion of a local Russian general." Churchill, *Triumph and Tragedy,* 514.

12. Eisenhower, *Crusade in Europe,* 396.

3

Eisenhower's Superiors and His Telegram to Stalin

FOLLOWING SEIZURE of the bridgehead at Remagen, Eisenhower's forces moved forward rapidly. By mid-March, Hodges had three corps of his First Army in the bridgehead and was astride the autobahn that led to Frankfurt. Patton's Third Army had jumped the Moselle River and closed to the Rhine, which it crossed on March 22 (to his delight, Patton got the Third Army across before Montgomery, whose preparations had been going on for weeks). Farther south, 6th Army Group was keeping pace and was prepared for the final campaign into southern Germany. To the north, 21st Army Group began its crossing on March 23–24; by the 28th Montgomery had secured a deep bridgehead and was prepared to exploit his victory. By the 28th also, 12th and 6th Army Groups had moved well eastward from the Rhine, Hodges' First Army having reached Marburg, while Patton, bypassing Frankfurt, had reached Lauterbach. Eisenhower's plans were to push 12th Army Group northeast and 21st Army Group southeast, so that they could meet in the Kassel-Paderborn area and isolate the Germans in the Ruhr. Once the junction was effected, they would reduce the Ruhr pocket and simultaneously turn eastward and overrun Germany.

On March 27, General Marshall wired Eisenhower from Washington to suggest that, with the imminent breakup of German defenses, the Supreme Commander might want to push heavy columns eastward on a broad front, on either the

Nuremberg-Linz or the Karlsruhe-Munich axis, in order to prevent the Germans from organizing resistance in the south. He
also raised the question of running into the Red Army. "One of
the problems which arises," Marshall said, "is that of meeting
the Russians. What are your ideas on control and coordination
to prevent unfortunate incidents and to sort out the two advancing forces? One possibility is an agreed line of demarcation. The
arrangements we now have with the Russians appear quite
inadequate for the situation you may face and it seems that
steps ought to be initiated without delay to provide for the
communication and liaison you will need with them during the
period when your forces may be mopping up in close proximity
or in contact with the Russian forces." On the same day, Montgomery wired Eisenhower to say that he was preparing to drive
for the Elbe River with the U.S. Ninth and the British Second
Army.[1]

The next day, Eisenhower made his decision. He wired
Montgomery, telling him that once the junction at Kassel-
Paderborn had been made U.S. Ninth Army would revert to
Bradley. 12th Army Group would then be responsible for
mopping up the Ruhr and for delivering the main offensive, on
the Erfurt-Leipzig-Dresden axis. Montgomery's mission would
be to protect Bradley's northern flank. Eisenhower then sent a
telegram to the Allied Military Missions to Moscow to be
passed on to Stalin, with a copy for the Combined Chiefs of
Staff. Eisenhower told Stalin of his plans to isolate the Ruhr,
said his next task would be to divide Germany by joining hands
with the Red Army, and declared that he intended to move eastward towards Dresden. "Before deciding firmly on my plans,"
he added, "it is, I think, most important they should be co-
ordinated as closely as possible with yours both as to direction
and timing. Could you, therefore, tell me your intentions and let

1. Marshall to Eisenhower, March 27, Eisenhower Mss., Box 53,
Montgomery to Eisenhower, March 27, Eisenhower Mss., Box 33, quoted
in Pogue, *The Supreme Command*, 434–35; Forrest Pogue, "The Decision to Halt at the Elbe," in Kent Roberts Greenfield, ed., *Command
Decisions* (Washington, 1960), 488.

me know how far the proposals outlined in this message conform to your probable action?" [2]

In order to understand the events which followed upon
Eisenhower's actions, it is necessary to digress briefly to consider the structure of the Allied Command, and the personal
relationships within it.

IF THE British-American alliance of World War II operated
more smoothly and efficiently than any in history, the primary
reason was that on the broadest issues the two nations agreed
upon their war aims. Common traditions and language also
helped, and so did the abilities of the men in command of the
fighting forces of the two nations. Another important factor was
the machinery through which the British and Americans worked
out their differences and decided upon their strategy, the Combined Chiefs of Staff.

The Combined Chiefs of Staff came into being in January,
1942.[3] Membership consisted of the chiefs of staff of the various arms in Britain and America plus the personal chiefs of
staff to the Prime Minister and to the President. The British already had an organization of their heads of services, the British
Chiefs of Staff; the Americans, to provide a parallel organization, created in early 1942 the Joint Chiefs of Staff. Obviously
the British Chiefs of Staff and the Joint Chiefs of Staff could not
meet regularly, as the individual members all had important
duties and functions in their own country. To provide a working
relationship for those periods when they were not meeting together, therefore, the Combined Chiefs of Staff set up perma-
nent headquarters in Washington. The British created in Washington a Joint Staff Mission, which communicated daily with the
British Chiefs of Staff and then presented British views to the

2. Eisenhower to Montgomery, March 28, Eisenhower Mss., Box
33; Eisenhower to Military Mission Moscow, Eisenhower Mss., Box 53;
quoted in John Toland, *The Last 100 Days* (New York, 1965), 308.

3. There is no history of the Combined Chiefs of Staff; one is
badly needed. The best discussion is Pogue, *The Supreme Command,* 36–
55, on which much of this account is based.

Joint Chiefs of Staff. For most of the war Field Marshal Sir
John Dill headed the Joint Staff Mission. The arrangement
worked without undue stress, primarily because Dill was a first-
rate diplomat and highly respected by the Americans, especially
Marshall. Unfortunately he died in November, 1944—the Amer-
icans showed their feelings toward him by burying him in
Arlington National Cemetery—to be succeeded by Sir Henry
Maitland Wilson. Field Marshal Wilson was competent enough,
but he simply was not Dill; it was rather like Jefferson replacing
Franklin as ambassador to France.

On occasion the system worked the other way round. The
Joint Chiefs of Staff would allow Eisenhower to represent them
before the British Chiefs of Staff with full authority to make
binding decisions on European matters. This cutting of corners
could save time in moments of crisis. It horrified the British,
who could not imagine delegating such authority to one of their
field commanders, but they were willing enough to accept the
American whim. The Joint Chiefs of Staff, uncomfortable with
the arrangement for another reason, did not use it very often.
They feared that the Supreme Commander would be unduly influenced by the views of the British. More than once Marshall
warned Eisenhower not to get too one-sided a view of Anglo-
American relations—he was aware of how greatly Eisenhower
admired the British, especially Churchill and General Hastings
Ismay, the Prime Minister's Chief of Staff—and he once asked
the British Chiefs of Staff not to place their views before the Supreme Commander until the matter had been taken up by the
full Combined Chiefs of Staff.

Under agreements reached in 1942, the Combined Chiefs of
Staff were responsible for all operations in Europe. Their agents
were the theater commanders, one for the Mediterranean and
another for Western Europe, who operated under their directive. The subordinates of a theater commander could not question his orders, even on nationalistic grounds. For example, if
Eisenhower gave Montgomery an order that Montgomery felt
would jeopardize British national interests, Montgomery had to

carry out the order. He could inform Eisenhower that he intended to protest to his own Chiefs of Staff, but he could not procrastinate.[4] The issue hardly ever arose, however, because both nations had full representation at the highest levels of theater command. The theater commander's staff was integrated, containing officers from both nations, and if the theater commander was an American his deputy was sure to be British. For administrative, supply, and personnel purposes the various officers remained responsible to their own services. Thus, on a question of American promotions, Eisenhower dealt directly with the U.S. Army Chief of Staff; on supply problems, the senior naval commander from the United States would go directly to the Chief of Naval Operations; to relieve a division commander, the senior British officer would by-pass the theater commander and consult with the Chief of the Imperial General Staff. On all operational questions, however, the theater commander was responsible to the Combined Chiefs of Staff, and subordinates in the field, no matter what their rank or nationality, were responsible to him.

The Combined Chiefs of Staff took their orders and directives from the heads of government. On most issues the chiefs would try to thrash out any difference between themselves and then present a united front to the Prime Minister and the President. Insofar as they were, collectively, the principal military advisers to the heads of government, when they did make a recommendation it was extremely difficult for Churchill and Roosevelt to disagree or overrule them. On a number of occasions, the North African landings of 1942 being the most notable, the Combined Chiefs of Staff could not agree; in such cases Churchill and Roosevelt had to find a compromise.

Roosevelt's dealings with the Joint Chiefs of Staff were

4. This was the major difference between Eisenhower's authority and that of Marshal Foch in 1918. It came about because Eisenhower insisted upon it when his first directive was written, in the summer of 1942 for the invasion of North Africa. See George F. Howe, *Northwest Africa: Seizing the Initiative in the West* (in Greenfield, ed., *United States Army in World War II*) (Washington, 1957), 16.

much different from Churchill's with the British Chiefs of Staff. In part, this was due to structural differences in the two systems. As commander in chief of all American armed forces, Roosevelt was in such an exalted position that he was nearly out of sight. He did not attend meetings of the Joint Chiefs of Staff (although his personal chief of staff, Admiral William D. Leahy, did, as a member, and presented the President's views), and hardly ever participated in any detailed discussions of operations. The coin had two sides to it; on political issues, such as the question of recognition of de Gaulle, he tended to ignore military advice and often did not even inform the Joint Chiefs of Staff of his decisions. Churchill's constitutional responsibilities required him to play a more active role in his relationship with the British Chiefs of Staff. As Minister of Defence, he regularly attended meetings of the British Chiefs of Staff; as an interested and often meddlesome observer, he kept in close contact with field commanders. While in North Africa, Eisenhower was shocked at the British practice of sending daily situational reports to London; he eventually got used to it, but never approved of it. Churchill enjoyed sending suggestions and criticisms to his generals, a practice which his Chiefs of Staff tried to get him to stop; the only result was that Churchill's wrath came down on their heads.

As far as the Supreme Commander in Europe was concerned, the most important members of the Combined Chiefs of Staff were Brooke and Marshall. As heads of the respective armies they were most intimately concerned with the ground battle and understood it best. They were the men to whom the heads of government looked for advice on developments in France and Germany. Eisenhower respected Brooke but was never close to him; their relationship was always coldly formal. By contrast, Eisenhower thought Marshall the greatest man he had ever met and trusted his judgment completely. Marshall had the deepest possible respect for Eisenhower and regarded him as something of a protégé. There was a father-son element in their relationship. Eisenhower knew that in a crisis he could always depend upon Marshall's support; he once said that this knowledge sustained him more than anything else through the war.

Eisenhower was in the States only once after June, 1942; Marshall made a few trips to Europe, but they were of short duration. The generals nevertheless kept each other fully informed of their views. As senior American officer in Europe, Eisenhower was responsible for administration of American troops in the theater; in this area he reported to and took his orders from Marshall. Furthermore, when Eisenhower communicated with the Combined Chiefs of Staff he did so through Marshall, and Marshall sent Combined Chiefs of Staff orders to the Supreme Commander. The two men exchanged daily telegrams. In addition, they frequently wrote personal letters to each other.

Through most of the war the Combined Chiefs of Staff system worked well. By the spring of 1945, however, it was beginning to break down. The two nations were no longer making a relatively equal contribution to the war effort; American preponderance had become so great that, if necessary, the Joint Chiefs of Staff were in a position to insist upon their judgment, while the British simply had to accept the decision in the best grace possible. Dill's death almost closed what had been an easy and open channel of communication. Most of all, the war was entering its final stages, the traditional time for alliances to disintegrate. As Henry A. Kissinger has written, "As long as the enemy is more powerful than any single member of the coalition, the need for unity outweighs all considerations of individual gain. Then the powers of repose can insist on the definition of war aims which, as all conditions, represent limitations. But when the enemy has been so weakened that each ally has the power to achieve its ends alone, a coalition is at the mercy of its most determined member. Confronted with the complete collapse of one of the elements of the equilibrium, all other powers will tend to raise their claims in order to keep pace." [5]

5. Henry A. Kissinger, *A World Restored* (new edition, New York, 1964), 109.

The stresses and strains within the Combined Chiefs of Staff system were most completely revealed by the events ensuing upon Eisenhower's telegram to Stalin. When the British Chiefs of Staff received their copy of the telegram, they were furious. On March 29 the Chiefs met; Brooke recorded their reaction in his diary. "A very long C.O.S. meeting with a series of annoying telegrams. The worst of all was one from Eisenhower direct to Stalin trying to co-ordinate his offensive with the Russians. To start with, he has no business to address Stalin direct, his communications should be through the Combined Chiefs of Staff; secondly, he produced a telegram which was unintelligible; and finally, what was implied in it appeared to be entirely adrift and a change from all that had been previously agreed on." Churchill sent a memorandum to Ismay saying, "This seems to differ from last night's Montgomery, who spoke of Elbe. Please explain." Neither Ismay nor any other member of the British Chiefs of Staff could explain, however, because they did not know that Eisenhower had taken Ninth Army away from Montgomery. They continued to assume that the main Allied drive would be in the north, under Montgomery's direction and headed for Berlin. When they learned the next day—from Montgomery, not Eisenhower—that Ninth Army would fight under Bradley, their irritation increased.[6]

The British were most concerned over the change in plan, but they were also upset at what they considered to be Eisenhower's exceeding his authority. They promptly proposed that the Allied Military Missions to Moscow be directed to hold up

6. Bryant, *Triumph in the West,* 336; Ehrman, *Grand Strategy,* 132–33. Montgomery was most unhappy. "I consider we are about to make a terrible mistake," he wired Brooke. "The great point now is speed of action, so that we can finish off German war in shortest possible time . . . SHAEF never seems to understand that, if you suddenly make big changes in Army Groups, you create confusion in signal arrangements and administration generally. My communications have been built up on assumption that Ninth Army would remain in 21 Army Group until we had cleared Northern Germany and this was declared intention of Eisenhower . . . It seems doctrine that public opinion wins wars is coming to the fore again." Bryant, *Triumph in the West,* 340–41.

delivery of later messages from Eisenhower to Stalin, and implied that Eisenhower ought to be censured for contacting a head of government directly. The Joint Chiefs of Staff emphatically rejected the proposal as one that would discredit the most successful field commander of the war. They were willing to ask Eisenhower to delay sending further messages to Moscow until he had consulted with the Combined Chiefs of Staff, but made it abundantly clear that it was unlikely they would interfere with Eisenhower's plans or conduct.[7]

For a soldier in the field to communicate directly with a head of government was unusual, but hardly unprecedented. Churchill often bypassed the Combined Chiefs of Staff to communicate directly with Eisenhower, and he had encouraged Eisenhower to come directly to him. Eisenhower was in constant communication with another head of government, Charles de Gaulle. At Yalta, Stalin had suggested that some arrangement be made to insure close co-ordination between Eisenhower's forces and the Red Army, and Roosevelt and Marshall had proposed that a direct liaison be created between SHAEF and the Soviet General Staff via the Allied Military Missions to Moscow. Churchill was reluctant to go along because he feared Eisenhower would then participate in decisions more properly left to political authorities. But Stalin and Roosevelt insisted, and Churchill agreed. It is true that they did not contemplate Eisenhower addressing himself to Stalin personally, but Eisenhower felt that in a fluid situation he had no choice, since all major decisions would be passed on to Stalin anyway and Eisenhower felt he could not afford to waste time.[8]

The chief result of this controversy was to anger the British. "The only other result," Eisenhower declared after the war, "was that we thereafter felt somewhat restricted in communicating with Stalin and were careful to confine all communications to matters of solely tactical importance. This situation I did not regard as too serious, particularly because the U.S. Chiefs of

7. Pogue, *The Supreme Command,* 441–42.
8. Feis, *Churchill, Roosevelt and Stalin,* 500–01, 603–04.

Staff had staunchly reaffirmed my freedom of action in execution of plans that in my judgment would bring about the earliest possible cessation of hostilities." [9]

The substantive issue was the question of the direction of the advance. The British Chiefs of Staff thought Eisenhower was making a grave mistake in advancing along the central rather than the northern route. In reply, the Joint Chiefs of Staff made a dig at British strategical insights by pointing out that Eisenhower's plan to fight the major battle west of the Rhine had been proved sound, even brilliant; they did not need to add that the British had opposed it. As to the future, the Joint Chiefs of Staff stated flatly that Eisenhower was "the best judge of the measures which offer the earliest prospect of destroying the German Armies or their power to resist," and added that his ideas were "sound from the overall viewpoint of crushing Germany as expeditiously as possible and should receive full support." [10]

The British Chiefs of Staff told the Joint Chiefs of Staff that Eisenhower's change of plan raised "issues which have a wider import than the destruction of the main enemy forces in Germany." Such language betrayed their concern that making a drive toward Dresden the main offensive meant that Berlin would be taken by the Russians. Churchill was quick to see that his military chiefs had laid themselves open to the charge of making a recommendation based on a political consideration. He called his chiefs on this point, saying that it seemed to him "a very odd phrase to be used in a Staff communication. I should have thought it laid itself open to a charge of extreme unorthodoxy." The Prime Minister, in short, did not want his soldiers meddling in political issues, and told them to keep their attention on "our usual line, . . . the destruction of the main enemy forces." [11] Churchill felt a good case could be made for the northern route on military grounds alone, and at this point

9. Eisenhower, *Crusade in Europe*, 403.
10. Pogue, *The Supreme Command*, 442.
11. Ehrman, *Grand Strategy*, 135–36.

he decided to eliminate the Combined Chiefs of Staff from the discussion by taking up the argument with Roosevelt.

The Prime Minister wired the President to point out that Eisenhower was not giving enough attention to northern Germany. The North Sea and Baltic ports, he said, could cause great trouble for the Allies and it was imperative to seize them quickly to prevent the renewal of submarine attacks. In addition, "I say quite frankly that Berlin remains of high strategic importance. Nothing will exert a psychological effect of despair upon all German forces of resistance equal to that of the fall of Berlin. It will be the supreme signal of defeat to the German people . . . To sum up, the difference that might exist between Eisenhower's plans and ours is Leipzig vs. Berlin. This is surely a matter upon which a reasonable latitude of discussion should be allowed before any final commitment involving the Russians is entered into."

Churchill then introduced, for the first time, the political argument. It revolved around the question of prestige. He said the Russians were going to liberate Vienna. "If they also take Berlin, will not their impression that they have been the overwhelming contributor to our common victory be unduly imprinted in their minds, and may this not lead them into a mood which will raise grave and formidable difficulties in the future? I therefore consider that from a political standpoint we should march as far east into Germany as possible and that should Berlin be in our grasp we should certainly take it. This also appears sound on military grounds." [12]

Churchill's argument was powerful, especially in retrospect. If the Cold War was inevitable, anything that could have forestalled the Russians in central Europe, even if only for a few weeks or months, or anything that could have taken from them some of the glory of victory, was worth trying. If, however, the Cold War was not inevitable—if there was any chance, however slight, of East-West co-operation after victory—then Berlin,

12. Churchill, *Triumph and Tragedy,* 464–65; Pogue, *The Supreme Command,* 442–43. See Appendix A for the full exchange of telegrams.

1945, was hardly the place to take a stand on "getting tough with the Russians." It seemed to Roosevelt that the possibility of co-operation was there, and since he had chosen to try and accommodate the Russians in Poland and over the German surrender in Italy, issues over which there was sharp Anglo-Russian disagreement, he was not going to change his policy in Berlin.

Churchill's position in the spring of 1945 was almost desperate. He personally remained a giant, an authentic member of the "Big Three." But his nation was not a great power; England could no longer stand alone. Churchill probably recognized that without a firm alliance with the United States the days of glory for the British Empire were over—and alliances have to be directed against someone. If he could persuade Roosevelt to assume a firm anti-Soviet posture, then England could, as a partner (albeit a junior one), continue to participate in the fundamental decisions of world politics. If, on the other hand, Roosevelt's dream of American-Russian co-operation through the agency of the United Nations came true, England's position would be very much weaker.

A. J. P. Taylor has suggested that Churchill felt in 1944 that Roosevelt was trying to slough him off while building closer ties with Stalin.[13] The Prime Minister tried to reverse this trend by inciting Roosevelt to indignation over Russian moves in Poland and elsewhere, but without success.

It may be that Churchill was simply taking the realistic position. The Prime Minister perhaps recognized that there never was the slightest possibility of East-West co-operation in the postwar world, and he wanted to make sure that the West emerged from the war in the strongest possible position. Roosevelt disagreed with this view, in what was his most important policy decision of the war, but he never had an opportunity to prove whether he was right or not. After his death, the new President, Harry S Truman, chose rather quickly after assum-

13 Taylor, *English History,* 574.

ing office to join Churchill in the anti-Soviet camp. This may have been the wise and perhaps only choice—it certainly seemed so to Truman and most of his advisers—but it does not prove that the Cold War was inevitable. The other approach did not have a fair trial.

For Eisenhower, these high level political decisions mattered little. His President had a policy, he knew what that policy was, and it was his duty to carry it out. By the same token it was Churchill's duty to try and change the President's mind.

Churchill had appealed directly to the President because he knew that Marshall, the dominant member of the Joint Chiefs of Staff, had such a high opinion of Eisenhower that he would never by himself interfere with the Supreme Commander's operations. But by this time Roosevelt was a sick man; Churchill discovered after the war that "the President's health was now so feeble that it was General Marshall who had to deal with these grave questions." Marshall probably drafted Roosevelt's reply, which stressed that the President could not see that Eisenhower had made any great changes in the agreed-upon strategy. Taking up another point that Churchill had raised, the President emphasized that Eisenhower was not underestimating the British contribution to victory nor did he wish to exclude 21st Army Group from the last campaign. In conclusion, Roosevelt's message said that the President regretted that "at the moment of a great victory we should become involved in such unfortunate reactions." [14]

On April 1 Eisenhower, in response to a telephone call from the Prime Minister, sent a full description of his plans to Churchill. He said he was "disturbed, if not hurt," at the suggestion that he was trying to relegate the British forces to a restricted sphere and assured the Prime Minister that "nothing is further from my mind and I think my record over two and one-half years of commanding Allied forces should eliminate any such idea." The Supreme Commander again explained his views

14. Churchill, *Triumph and Tragedy,* 465; Pogue, *The Supreme Command,* 443.

in full (he had done so two days earlier), telling the Prime Minister that he was merely trying to defeat Germany as fast as possible. He did not feel that he had made any important strategical changes, and he had not yet made a final decision about Berlin.[15]

The British insisted that there had been a change (even if to save face they eventually shrugged it off as a "minor" one); the confusion was due to preconceived notions. Eisenhower's objective had always been the German army, and in that sense his plans never changed. The British saw Berlin as the objective. Until Remagen this fundamental difference in outlook was unimportant, because until then Eisenhower felt he could most quickly destroy the German army by attacking in strength along the northern route. Partly because of what happened at Remagen and after, partly because the German strength shifted southwards, Eisenhower redirected his advance. To his mind this did not represent a change; to the British it did.

Eisenhower's feelings about Berlin differed from those of the British. When Montgomery protested the removal of Ninth Army and said it would make it impossible for him to get Berlin, Eisenhower declared "that place has become, so far as I am concerned, nothing but a geographical location, and I have never been interested in these. My purpose is to destroy the enemy's forces and his powers to resist." [16] As his chief of staff later explained, "Battles are fought to defeat armies, to destroy the enemy's ability to go on fighting. Only when a port, such as Cherbourg, or an area, such as the Ruhr, is so vital to the enemy that it is protected with large numbers of troops, or when a particular locality . . . provides great advantages for the further development of a campaign, are 'terrain objectives' of justified military importance." With the German government gone from the capital, "Berlin was a terrain objective empty of mean-

15. Eisenhower to Churchill, April 1, Eisenhower Mss., Box 13, quoted in Pogue, *The Supreme Command,* 443.
16. Eisenhower to Montgomery, March 31, Eisenhower Mss., Box 33, quoted in Toland, *The Last 100 Days,* 325.

ing." Under the circumstances, "to send our armies crashing into its western suburbs could have no tactical significance." [17]

Eisenhower's communications with the British were calm and straightforward. His irritation at having his plans questioned, however, was growing; he let some of it show in a cable to Marshall. He was, he said, "completely in the dark as to what the protest concerning 'procedure' involved. I have been instructed to deal directly with the Russians concerning military coordination." As for his strategy, Eisenhower insisted he had made no changes. "The British Chiefs of Staff last summer always protested against my determination to open up the [central] . . . route because they said it would be futile and . . . draw strength away from a northern attack." He had, however, "always insisted that the northern attack would be the principal effort" until the Ruhr was isolated, "but from the very beginning, extending back before D-Day, my plan . . . has been to link up . . . primary and secondary efforts . . . and then make one great thrust to the eastward. Even cursory examination . . . shows that the principal effort should . . . be toward the Leipzig region, in which area is concentrated the greater part of the remaining German industrial capacity and to which area German ministries are believed to be moving."

Recalling the old British argument for a single thrust, Eisenhower declared, "Merely following the principle that Field Marshal Brooke has always shouted to me, I am determined to concentrate on one major thrust and all that my plan does is to place the Ninth U.S. Army back under Bradley for that phase of operations involving the advance of the center . . ." The Supreme Commander reiterated his conclusion that "Berlin itself is no longer a particularly important objective. Its usefulness to the German has been largely destroyed and even his government is preparing to move to another area. What is now important is to gather up our forces for a single drive, and this will more quickly bring about the fall of Berlin, the relief of Norway and

17. Smith, *Eisenhower's Six Great Decisions,* 186.

the acquisition of the shipping and the Swedish ports than will the scattering around of our effort."

In his last paragraph Eisenhower made no attempt to hide his feelings. "The Prime Minister and his Chiefs of Staff opposed ANVIL; they opposed my idea that the German should be destroyed west of the Rhine before we made our great effort across the river; and they insisted that the route leading northeastward from Frankfurt would involve us merely in slow, rough-country fighting. Now they apparently want me to turn aside on operations in which would be involved many thousands of troops before the German forces are fully defeated. I submit that these things are studied daily and hourly by me and my advisors and that we are animated by one single thought which is the early winning of the war." [18]

Churchill ended the controversy on April 5 by wiring the President. "I still think it was a pity that Eisenhower's telegram was sent to Stalin without anything being said to our Chiefs of Staff," he declared. "The changes in the main plan have now turned out to be very much less than we at first supposed. My personal relations with General Eisenhower are of the most friendly character. I regard the matter as closed, and to prove my sincerity I will use one of my very few Latin quotations: *Amantium irae amoris integratio est.*" [19]

Meanwhile Eisenhower's elucidation of his plans had helped calm down the British Chiefs of Staff. At an April 1 meeting at Chequers, the Prime Minister's country estate, the chiefs discussed the entire problem. Brooke was mollified because "it is quite clear that there is no very great change," but still irritated because "most of the changes are due to national aspirations and to ensure that the U.S. effort will not be lost under British command. It is all a pity and straightforward strategy is being affected by the nationalistic outlook of allies. This is one of the

18. Eisenhower to Marshall, March 31, Eisenhower Mss., Box 53, quoted in Ryan, *The Last Battle,* 237–39.

19. Churchill, *Triumph and Tragedy,* 468. The War Department translation read, "Lovers quarrels are a part of love." Pogue, *The Supreme Command,* 444.

handicaps of operating with allies. But, as Winston says, 'there is only one thing worse than fighting with allies, and that is fighting without them!' " [20] The British agreed, in short, that they would no longer dispute 21st Army Group's role in the final campaign. The question of Berlin remained open.

A major result of the dispute was the way it brought into the open the new nature of the Combined Chiefs of Staff. No longer was it an agency of equals in which strategy was hammered out through the process of give and take. What the Americans wanted, if they wanted it badly enough, they got. The Joint Chiefs of Staff domination of the Combined Chiefs of Staff reflected, in turn, a new era in the world's history. The United States had replaced Great Britain as the dominant power bordering on the Atlantic Ocean. By 1945 American production had reached levels that were scarcely believable. The United States was producing 45 per cent of the world's armament and nearly 50 per cent of the world's goods. Some two-thirds of all the ships afloat in the world were American-made.

In 1942, when the British were making the largest contribution to the alliance and the Combined Chiefs of Staff reached a deadlock, the British were able to insist upon their view and the alliance committed its strength to the Mediterranean. In late 1943, when the two nations were making a fairly equal contribution and the Combined Chiefs of Staff reached a deadlock, it took a third party—Stalin—to break it, and the alliance committed its strength to OVERLORD. In 1945, when the Americans were making the largest contribution and there was a deadlock, the Americans insisted upon their view and it was carried out.

At one point during the Berlin debate, Churchill had to remind Brooke of something that Marshall was well aware of— the British contribution to Allied resources was down to 25 per cent of the whole. If the British Chiefs of Staff disapproved of a proposed action on which the Americans felt strongly. they

20. Bryant, *Triumph in the West*. 339.

could only turn to Churchill for help, in the hope that he could turn Roosevelt against the Joint Chiefs.

The President, who had on a few previous occasions gone along with Churchill and in the process overruled the Joint Chiefs, refused to do so this time. His health is one possible reason (and the one that Churchill cited in his memoirs); but not enough is presently known on the exact state of Roosevelt's health to make this more than a speculation. Through the war the Joint Chiefs' influence in general and Marshall's in particular had grown; Roosevelt was increasingly inclined to accept his advisers' views. The Churchill-Roosevelt relationship was showing signs of strain, and after Roosevelt met Stalin at Teheran and later at Yalta Churchill's influence on the President had waned. But most of all, Churchill's attempt to swing Roosevelt over to his side failed because the President had a different policy. He was not ready to start an anti-Communist crusade; he did want to end the war quickly, and he backed his military leaders in their plans to give him a speedy victory.

The Joint Chiefs of Staff felt Eisenhower had conducted the campaign up to and across the Rhine in masterful fashion, and they were not willing to interfere with him. This was especially true when Eisenhower's wishes were firm and well known, as they were in this case. "So earnestly did I believe in the military soundness of what we were doing," Eisenhower declared later, "that my intimates on the staff knew I was prepared to make an issue of it." [21] So vivid were his telegrams to Washington on the subject that the Joint Chiefs of Staff knew it too. Under the circumstances they decided that the British would have to save face the best they could, for the Joint Chiefs of Staff would not allow the Combined Chiefs of Staff to question the Supreme Commander's policies.

On April 6 the Joint Chiefs of Staff made their position absolutely clear to the British Chiefs of Staff. "Only Eisenhower is in a position to know how to fight his battle, and to exploit to the full the changing situation," they said. Even if they wanted

21. Eisenhower, *Crusade in Europe,* 403.

to interfere, they would not in this case, because they agreed with the Supreme Commander's assessment of the situation. On Berlin, the Joint Chiefs of Staff declared that such "psychological and political advantages as would result from the possible capture of Berlin ahead of the Russians should not override the imperative military consideration, which in our opinion is the destruction and dismemberment of the German armed forces." [22]

The next day Eisenhower told the Combined Chiefs of Staff that once he reached the Elbe River he planned to clear out his northern and southern flanks. If after those operations were concluded he could still take Berlin, well and good. He insisted that his judgments were made purely on military grounds, and declared that he would need in effect a new directive if the Combined Chiefs of Staff wished him to operate on political grounds. "I regard it as militarily unsound at this stage of the proceedings to make Berlin a major objective, particularly in view of the fact that it is only 35 miles from the Russian lines," he said.

Then Eisenhower added, "I am the first to admit that a war is waged in pursuance of political aims, and if the Combined Chiefs of Staff should decide that the Allied effort to take Berlin outweighs purely military considerations in this theater, I would cheerfully readjust my plans and my thinking so as to carry out such an operation." [23] If, in short, Churchill was prepared to make Russia instead of Germany the enemy, and if he could get Roosevelt to agree, Eisenhower would willingly change his plans, for then the military considerations would be much different.

The Combined Chiefs of Staff did not even discuss Eisenhower's cable or the question of Berlin,[24] and the final decision came down to Eisenhower. His thoughts and his plans were all that counted.

22. Pogue, "Decision to Halt," *op. cit.,* 485–86.
23. Eisenhower to Marshall, April 7, Eisenhower Mss., Box 53; quoted in *ibid.,* 486.
24. William D. Leahy, *I Was There* (New York, 1950), 303.

4

The Military Situation
and the Basis
for Decision

"We want a *Feldherr* who will make war, not one who is a politician," Metternich declared in 1814 as the allies closed in on Napoleon.[1] So it has always been. The civilian heads of government, whether in a monarchy, a democracy, a totalitarian dictatorship, or any other form of government, wish to make the political decisions. Well aware of the political implications of his movements, Eisenhower was nevertheless determined whenever possible to carry on his operations in strict accordance with military requirements.

The first factor in the military situation was the Russian position and intentions. On February 15 the Russians had reached the Oder-Neisse line, some thirty-five miles from Berlin. They were faced by two German armies and had flat, dry land between them and the city. For the next month and a half they built up their position in preparation for the final assault; by early April Marshal Zhukov, on the Oder River, had 768,100 men and 11,000 artillery pieces, not counting smaller-caliber mortars. Marshal Koniev, on the Neisse River, had five field and two tank armies with artillery equal to Zhukov's. The total strength of the Red Army around Berlin was 1,250,000 men and 22,000 guns.[2] (SHAEF's *total* ground strength at this

1. Gordon A. Craig, *Problems of Coalition Warfare: The Military Alliance Against Napoleon, 1813–1814* (U.S. Air Force Academy, Colorado, 1965), 5.
2. Ryan, *The Last Battle*, 251.

time, including troops still in England, was less than 2,400,-
000). Zhukov and Koniev had what must be reckoned as the
greatest armed force in so small an area in the whole of military
history. Although Eisenhower did not know the exact figures, he
did realize that the Russians had an enormous force ready to
strike for Berlin at a time when his troops were just completing
the Ruhr encirclement and were 250 miles from the city. It was,
on the face of it, foolish to even think about, much less plan on,
racing the Russians to Berlin.

Concerned with ending the war as soon as possible, Eisenhower believed that the best way to accomplish this was to drive
through to Dresden, linking up with the Russians as soon as
possible. Once Eisenhower had joined with the Red Army to
split Germany in half, mopping-up operations could be carried
out. The German communications network would be badly
hurt, if not destroyed, by the division; German troops from one
area could not reinforce those in another; organization in general would be gone.

Stalin strengthened Eisenhower's views when he replied to
Eisenhower's March 28 telegram. Stalin said he agreed that Ber-
lin no longer was of any great importance and that therefore the
Red Army would make its main thrust toward Dresden.[3] The
allies would split Germany in half by rushing forward toward
Dresden.

The central axis had another appeal for Eisenhower. An
attack toward Dresden would be directed by Bradley, and since
the capture of the Ludendorff Bridge at Remagen the Supreme

3. In the event, the Red Army made its major thrust somewhat to
the north of Dresden and a little to the south of Berlin. Ryan contends
that Stalin all along intended to drive to Berlin and deliberately lied
to Eisenhower. There is evidence to indicate that Stalin or his field commanders merely changed plans in the middle of the battle in response
to shifting conditions. No one in the West knows for sure, since the
Russian documents have not been made available. The point here is that
Eisenhower believed the Red Army would be heading for Dresden. See
Ryan, *The Last Battle*, 243, and Stephen E. Ambrose, "Refighting the
Last Battle—The Pitfalls of Popular History," *Wisconsin Magazine of
History*, XLIX (Summer, 1966).

Commander's opinion of Bradley had gone ever higher. On March 28 he wired Marshall to say of Bradley, "He has never once held back in attempting any maneuver, no matter how bold in conception and never has he paused to regroup when there was opportunity lying on his front. His handling of his army commanders has been superb and his energy, common-sense, tactical skill and complete loyalty have made him a great lieutenant on whom I can always rely with the greatest confidence. I consider Bradley the greatest battle-line commander I have met in this war." The next day Eisenhower told Marshall that Hodges, whose First Army would lead the way to Dresden, was his best army commander. Of Hodges he said that from the end of February, "his drive, clear-headed and tactical skill have shone even more brightly than they did in his great pursuit across France, in which First Army's part was the most difficult given to any United States formation but brilliantly and speedily executed, often against much resistance." [4]

Obviously, he believed that these two generals would do the best job of winning the war quickly. But there was something else involved. Eisenhower was as conscious of public relations as any soldier in history. He knew that his troops liked to feel that their efforts were being appreciated on the home front, and that the criteria they used to judge was newspaper headlines. Unfortunately, since D-Day, most of the headlines had gone to either Patton or Montgomery. Furthermore, whenever Patton's or Montgomery's troops did something spectacular the generals, with whom the troops identified, were mentioned by name in the headlines. But when Hodges' men captured an important point, the headline ran, "First Army Takes . . ." This had led to some jealousy in the Allied armies directed against Patton and Montgomery.

This jealousy was most keenly felt in First Army, which had the dirtiest and roughest tasks throughout the campaign, but which seldom had an opportunity to do something spectacular.

4. Eisenhower to Marshall, March 28 and 29, Eisenhower Mss., Box 53, quoted in Pogue, *The Supreme Command,* 435.

Eisenhower had tried, time and again, to get the public relations officers in Washington to persuade the newspapers to give some space to Hodges and First Army (and to General William Simpson's Ninth Army), but without success. Eisenhower told Marshall in late March that he felt First Army's work had been overlooked and that others had received credit for accomplishments actually gained by Bradley and Hodges. By giving the last offensive to them, Eisenhower felt he could correct the situation.

The concentration on the center would accomplish other objectives for Eisenhower. With U.S. Ninth Army on Bradley's left, 21st Army Group was free to turn further north and drive for Lübeck on the Baltic (if Ninth Army stayed with Montgomery and 21st Army Group headed for Berlin, the north coast would be neglected). The drive to Lübeck would cut off German troops in the Danish peninsula and the occupation forces in Norway, Germany's last major source of reserves. An incidental advantage, mentioned by Eisenhower at the time, was that it would keep the Russians out of Denmark, which of course had not been assigned to any of the allies for occupation purposes. An attack toward Lübeck would gain the north coast ports of Bremen and Hamburg, thereby easing the supply and communications situation and reducing the submarine menace.[5] Finally, it would starve out the Germans in Norway. Eisenhower was afraid of prolonged resistance in the mountain areas of that country, a fear that was increased by the fanatical resistance of German troops cut off in the Netherlands and various French port cities.

If Eisenhower's actions were geared to winning the war as soon as possible, the question must be raised: why? What factors made speed so important? The answer involves many facets, but by far the most important was the simplest—this was his job. He was supposed to win as decisively as he could as soon as he could.

Beyond that requirement, Eisenhower knew that the Ameri-

5. *Ibid.*, 435–36; Eisenhower, *Crusade in Europe*, 397.

can and even more the British people were tired of the war and
wanted it ended. No soldier or politician could have justified
any operation that prolonged the agony. In addition, as Allied
troops uncovered the concentration camps and the full horror of
the Nazi regime was revealed, hatred of the enemy increased in
intensity. Public opinion in both the United States and Great
Britain would have exploded at any hint of substituting the Russians for the Germans as the chief enemy. The English-speaking
world wanted the Germans punished for their unspeakable
crimes.

There was another factor. The United States had put by far
its major effort into the European war, but many American citi-
zens were more concerned with the war in the Pacific. There
was always a strong feeling in the United States, encouraged by
General Douglas MacArthur and some senior Navy officers,
that the country should turn away from Europe and concentrate
on Japan. By April, 1945, the United States was eager to get
the war in Germany over with as soon as possible in order to
redeploy the troops to the Pacific. Eisenhower was under constant and great pressure to accomplish this goal, and his staff was
working on redeployment plans long before the war ended. Had
Eisenhower gone across the Elbe toward Berlin and ignored the
Germans to the south and north, it is possible that the Nazis
could have stretched out the war by a few months. To SHAEF,
and to nearly every other observer, it seemed a certainty that
this would happen.

Had the war in Europe dragged on, causing a delay in redeployment, there could have been incalculable results. Japan was
still very much in the fight, and the invasion of the home is-
lands, in itself a frightening prospect, was more than a half-year
away. MacArthur needed all the troops he could get, and Marshall wanted to give them to him. The war could not end until
Japan was defeated, and even with the most rapid transfer of
troops the most optimistic estimate on Japanese defeat was the
spring of 1946. The Russian promise to declare war on Japan
within three months of the defeat of Germany helped some, but
by itself it would not be enough. And since the date of Russian

entry was dependent upon the end of the war in Germany, this was another factor pushing Eisenhower toward a quick conclusion in Europe. The atomic bomb has helped everyone to forget these possibilities, but in April, 1945, it had not yet been tested. At that time Americans at all levels and stations agreed that the prime necessity was to get troops to the Pacific.

Eisenhower was also concerned about the possible effects of prolonged German resistance on the grand alliance. From 1943 on, the Allies had feared that the Germans would quit only as corpses. As soon as the Wehrmacht went on the defensive, Hitler demonstrated, on every front, his fortress psychology. From the soldier's point of view he was a madman whose actions, especially in the last stages of the campaign, had no connection with reality. But his madness was not without cunning; he was capable of organizing skillful defensive systems that took time and lives to overrun. And the German troops showed that they could put up a fanatical resistance.

The most Hitler could buy with his fortresses was time, but that was exactly what the Allies could not afford to let him have. Not only was there the Japanese war to think about, there was also the frightening possibility of new secret weapons. Germany had made rapid strides in military technology during the war, German propaganda continued to urge the people to hold on just a little longer until the new weapons were ready, and the Allies knew that most experimental labs and some production facilities were underground where the air forces could not get at them. The V-weapons, jet-propelled airplanes and snorkel submarines were bad enough; no one knew what else the Germans might be working on. Finally, a delay in the end of the war was dangerous because of the possibility of an East-West split, signs of which appeared in April over Poland and over the surrender of German forces in Italy. A costly siege of prepared defensive positions might involve Russia and the West in disagreements through which the Germans "might yet be able to secure terms more favorable than unconditional surrender." [6]

6. Ehrman, *Grand Strategy*, 133.

The Germans had not given up the fight; there is no evidence to indicate, for example, that they slacked off in the West while increasing their efforts in the East in order to allow Great Britain and the United States to occupy their country. They still counted on a falling out between East and West, and there was even wild talk in Berlin about joining hands with the Western Allies to drive the Russians back to the Volga. Hitler and his cohorts were sure that Churchill, if not Roosevelt, was uncomfortable over the idea of the Russians pouring into central Europe. At worst the two sides would soon begin bickering over the spoils, at best begin World War III when they met in Berlin.[7] Meanwhile the Nazis would hold on—time was with them. Eisenhower was determined to prevent this falling out. The best way to do it was to overrun Germany quickly and force an unconditional surrender.

The demand for unconditional surrender was a political one with which Eisenhower did not agree but to which his nation was committed. He could do nothing about that. In any case, he wanted a clear-cut surrender that would be easily en-

7. Lord Ismay puts this, and other matters, into clear perspective. He writes: "Those who now aspire to prescribe what ought to have been done, must in fairness bear in mind the circumstances of those days. For over three years, public opinion in America and Britain had been led to believe that Russia was a brave and faithful ally who had done the lion's share of the fight, and endured untold suffering. If their Governments had now proclaimed that the Russians were untrustworthy and unprincipled tyrants, whose ambitions must be held in check, the effect on national unity in both countries would have been catastrophic. And if the British and American Governments had pushed the matter to extremes, and threatened to oppose the Soviet by force, what was to be done about the two to three hundred German divisions which the Germans still maintained in the field? Should Britain and America have continued to fight the Wehrmacht with one hand and the Red Army with the other? Or should they have forgotten all that they had said about their determination to destroy Nazism, taken the Germans into their fold, and proceeded, with their help, to crush their recent allies? One is forced to the conclusion that such a reversal of policy, which dictators could have taken in their stride, was absolutely impossible for the leaders of democratic countries even to contemplate." Ismay, *Memoirs*, 392.

forceable throughout Germany. Because the war did end with such a surrender, it is easy enough in retrospect to forget the alternatives, but in early 1945 they were very much alive in the minds of officers at SHAEF. Guerrilla warfare was not a new phenomenon, but it had reached impressive new heights of efficiency during World War II. SHAEF knew that the Germans were organizing an underground army of "Werewolves," youngsters who were being trained for murder and terrorism. The SS provided them with leadership, weapons, and fanaticism. If the Germans had time enough to perfect the organization and training, they could at the least make the occupation so costly that the conquering forces might be glad to get out. "The evidence was clear that the Nazi intended to make the attempt and I decided to give him no opportunity to carry it out," Eisenhower later declared. "The way to stop this project . . , was to overrun the entire national territory before its organization could be effected." [8]

As will be seen, SHAEF intelligence allowed itself to be overwhelmed by these fears. We know now that the Germans never mounted any serious guerrilla activities behind the lines, nor did any of their garrisons attempt to hold out after the general surrender. SHAEF did not know that in 1945. Still, the evidence was there, and with better intelligence work (or perhaps a calmer situation) the real picture could have been seen. There are a number of prerequisites to successful guerrilla warfare, none of which were available to the Germans in 1945. Guerrilla bands need supplies and equipment; the Germans did not have even enough for their regular forces, and did not have an air force which could drop material even if material were available. Partisans are not subject to the rigid discipline of regular forces; they must have a strong ideological commitment *and* a firm belief in eventual victory to bear the hardships their life necessarily involves. In 1945 few Germans had the commitment and hardly any had the belief. Guerrillas need the support

8. Eisenhower, *Crusade in Europe,* 397.

of the local population; to get it they must convince the people that their side will someday return and their government rule the area (in both France and Russia, guerrilla activity became significant only when the tide turned and it was clear that de Gaulle's Free French and Stalin's Red Army would be back). In April, 1945, it would have been difficult indeed to convince any German that Hitler would return. All these considerations apply with equal force to isolated garrisons, such as Leningrad or Stalingrad. None of these factors were present in Germany in 1945; the soil there was not a fruitful one for guerrilla or fortress activity. The real objective was the German regular army, not partisans lurking in the shadows.

Still SHAEF intelligence feared, and found evidence to support its fear. From early March on, it claimed that most SS divisions were moving toward a mountain stronghold around Berchtesgaden. This was easily the best natural defensive region the Germans could find; in the Bavarian Alps the Germans could combine the fighting forces from Germany and Italy.

Even Churchill felt this was a real possibility. On March 17 he asked Ismay to comment on Hitler's strategy, which puzzled the Prime Minister. "The strange resistance Hitler made at Budapest and is now making at Lake Balaton," Churchill felt, made sense only if the Nazis were planning to retire into southern Germany in an attempt to prolong the fighting there.[9] To American and Russian intelligence, this was the only explanation for the transfer of Sixth SS Panzer Army to the Danube Valley *after* the Russians had arrived on the Oder River.[10]

The SHAEF G-2 estimates were frightening. On February 16, Allied spies in Switzerland had sent to Washington a report obtained from sources in Berlin: "The Nazis are undoubtedly preparing for a bitter fight from the mountain redoubt . . . Strongpoints are connected by underground railroads . . . several months' output of the best munitions have

9. Feis, *Churchill, Roosevelt, and Stalin,* 594; Churchill, *Triumph and Tragedy,* 457.
10. Wilmot, *Struggle for Europe,* 690.

been reserved and almost all of Germany's poison gas supplies. Everybody who participated in the construction of the secret installations will be killed off—including the civilians who happen to remain behind . . . when the real fighting starts."

As early as March 11 SHAEF G-2 had summed up all the rumors. "The main trend of German defence policy does seem directed primarily to the safeguarding of the Alpine Zone. This area is, by the very nature of the terrain, practically impenetrable . . . The evidence indicates that considerable numbers of SS and specially chosen units are being systematically withdrawn to Austria . . . and that some of the most important ministries and personalities of the Nazi regime are already established in the Redoubt area." The reporter, carried away with his own verbiage, continued, "Here, defended by nature and by the most efficient secret weapons yet invented, the powers that have hitherto guided Germany will survive to reorganize her resurrection, here armaments will be manufactured in bombproof factories, food and equipment will be stored in vast underground caverns and a specially selected corps of young men will be trained in guerrilla warfare, so that a whole underground army can be fitted and directed to liberate Germany from the occupying forces." [11] The summary must rank as one of the worst intelligence reports of all time.

SHAEF began flying reconnaissance missions over the area. The results were confusing. The Germans seemed to be installing extensive bunkers, and there was a definite increase in antiaircraft protection. There was, however, no pattern to the construction. Increased activity in villages and towns indicated that each was being converted into a separate fortress, and rumors had it that Munich, western gateway to the area, was being made into a fortress which would be fought for street by street. Supposedly the preparations there exceeded any defenses set up in Berlin. In addition to all this, the Germans were known to have about 50 divisions north of the line on which the Russians and Americans would link up, with 100 to the south. The bulk

11. *Ibid.,* 690.

of the remaining armored and SS formations were concentrated in the south, which to General Walter Bedell Smith, Eisenhower's Chief of Staff, "gave added importance to seizing the National Redoubt before its defenses could be fully developed." [12] The danger seemed clear. Even as late as April 24, Bradley told some touring Congressmen that "we may be fighting one month from now and it may even be a year." When some of the visitors looked alarmed, Bradley told them of his apprehensions of a lingering campaign in the redoubt.[13]

Since there never was a redoubt, never any prepared positions, never any firm German plan to move troops into the region (although because of the pressure from their enemies they did tend to drift in that direction), the whole thing seems to have been a horrible mistake.[14] SHAEF intelligence has been frequently and vigorously criticized for accepting the story of the redoubt. Actually, the mistakes of the G-2 work are understandable. Most intelligence reports emphasized that there was no hard information available. It did seem likely that the fanatical Nazis would make a last ditch stand somewhere, and there was no better place to make it. In any case, and this is the crux of the matter, even if no fortifications had been erected the area would have been extremely difficult to capture—if the Germans could organize a garrison defense there. Natural defenses were excellent; the persistently bad weather, the mountainous terrain, and the altitude would have cut down on or eliminated the use of air forces; the Germans had convincingly demonstrated in Italy how well they could fight in mountains; the Allies' most potent weapon, their mobility, would have counted for little in the area.

Eisenhower could not safely disregard his G-2 reports. SHAEF intelligence estimates were based on information gathered from the armies and the army groups, from resistance

12. Smith, *Eisenhower's Six Great Decisions,* 188.
13. Bradley, *A Soldier's Story,* 536.
14. On the myth of the redoubt, see Rodney G. Minott, *The Fortress That Never Was* (New York, 1964).

groups, from the Office of Strategic Services and the Political Warfare Executive, from the War and Navy Departments in Washington, and from the Joint Intelligence Committee in London. SHAEF intelligence tended to be two or three days slow, and its record at the time of the Battle of the Bulge indicated that it was far from perfect. Nevertheless, Eisenhower would have been foolish to ignore his G-2 presentations,[15] and in view of these reports and of his objectives, it was inevitable that he would so shape his campaign as to prevent the build-up in south Germany of a strong force. From his point of view, it did not matter whether defenses there were prepared or not; in a very real sense they had been prepared centuries ago when the mountains were formed. They were just waiting for their garrison.

The extent to which the fear of a mountain stronghold influenced his plans was best revealed by his Chief of Staff, General Smith, in a press conference on April 21. Smith began with a statement on the general situation. "Now let's get down to cases," he continued, "and talk about two or three things . . . This so-called 'national redoubt' is something we don't know an awful lot about." SHAEF did know that troops and supplies were being moved into the area. "Just what we will find down there we don't know. We are beginning to think it will be a lot more than we expect." Smith reminded the reporters of the underground installations around Schweinfurt, "where we have been just bombing the hell out of the ballbearing plants and doing a marvelous job of hitting buildings, and finding eighty-five per cent were underground, beautifully underground." He expected that most plants in the mountains were also underground.

SHAEF had made the redoubt a target. Bradley was going to start his troops for it the next morning. Smith hoped that Bradley could drive a deep wedge into the area, so "that we will prevent any further organization, and that we will so disrupt it that the thing will end up reasonably quickly." He expected that

15. The best account of SHAEF G-2 is Pogue, *The Supreme Command,* 71–72.

once the mountains were overrun the Germans in the isolated garrisons around Europe—in Denmark, Norway, Holland, and the French ports—would give up. "That is why I say that the center, that is, the so-called 'thrust on Berlin,' from a purely military standpoint has ceased to be of any great importance to us. Berlin is going to fall, anyway. We don't care who fights their way into Berlin." Smith knew that the reporters had been "asking why we haven't pushed like hell toward Berlin." The answer was simple: "From a purely military standpoint it doesn't have much significance any more—not anything comparable to that of the so-called national redoubt and a jumping-off place from which later we can operate in Norway if we have to, and we have oriented our strength in that direction."

During the question period one reporter wanted to know if "it will be a very difficult job reducing the national redoubt?" Smith said he did not think so. "A month's fighting and then guerrilla warfare for an indeterminate time. That is not to be quoted. I don't know. That is only a guess." In reply to another question Smith said he had no firm information on the whereabouts of Hitler. As a wild guess he would say he thought Hitler was at Berchtesgaden, organizing the defense. A reporter asked if there was any chance of an airborne operation on Berchtesgaden. "We are keeping airborne divisions available," Smith replied. "We will have all sorts of airborne operations." Another newspaper man wanted to know if Smith had any reports on new German weapons. "We get constant rumors," he replied, "but nothing that would give us any really definite information. They are always threatening things and there may be something to them."

Would the Russians participate in the reduction of the national redoubt? "I have no doubt they will," Smith declared. "They are as anxious as we are to clear it." Was there any indication about Russian intentions toward Berlin while the Allied Expeditionary Force moved into southern Germany? "They said they'd make a secondary effort toward Berlin."

"Secondary?" the reporter asked.

"When you consider the number of divisions the Russians dispose," Smith replied, "a secondary effort would be a damn strong thing. Now you are asking my personal opinion—they will make a hell of an effort and take the place." [16]

Smith was being perfectly honest with the reporters, an action typical of him and of SHAEF. Eisenhower in particular and SHAEF in general usually enjoyed a "good press" because of their openness and straightforwardness with the newspaper men. The reporters, and through them the world, now knew what SHAEF intended to do, and why.

But despite Smith's honesty at the time there has been a great deal of confusion on the point. Critics have complained that Eisenhower swallowed the myth of a redoubt, that this was his sole reason for turning south when he reached the Elbe River, and that this mistaken reading of German intentions was the primary cause of his greatest failure. In fact, Eisenhower and SHAEF were always perfectly willing to admit that they did not know exactly what was going on in the redoubt area, and to point out that there were many, many reasons for not concentrating everything on a thrust through to Berlin while leaving the remainder of Germany alone.

A large number of factors influenced Eisenhower's decision. The possibility of the existence of a prepared redoubt was one, but only one, of them. Much more important was the general fear, encouraged by SHAEF intelligence, of prolonged garrison resistance and guerrilla warfare.[17] This illogical but real fear, which colored much of Eisenhower's thinking on operations both in the south and elsewhere, was in many people's minds. Churchill shared it. The Prime Minister thought the way to prevent such German action was to take Berlin because of the psychological effect it would have on the Germans. Eisenhower felt

16. Harry C. Butcher, *My Three Years With Eisenhower* (New York, 1946), 809–15.

17. The head of intelligence at SHAEF, British General Kenneth W. D. Strong, put SHAEF's point of view most succinctly when he said, "The redoubt may not be there, but we have to take steps to prevent it being there." Ryan, *The Last Battle,* 214.

that the way to accomplish this purpose was to overrun all of
Germany; in any case, the psychological effect of the fall of Berlin on the Germans would be the same whether the city fell to
the East or the West.

Beyond these considerations, it was imperative for Eisenhower to arrange for an orderly, safe meeting with the Red
Army. Most soldiers worry incessantly about the possibility of
an accidental clash between allied troops. Fighting men can
make themselves endure most inconveniences and even accus-
tom themselves to death, when they are sure it serves a useful
purpose. Nothing, however, destroys morale more quickly than
seeing friends and comrades killed by friendly forces, whether it
be by "shorts" from an air bombardment along the front lines or
in a collision with allied forces.[18] The chances were great because of the unfamiliar uniforms and the language differences.
Further, Bradley and Eisenhower had been given to understand
that the Russians "had grown increasingly cocky and rash with
each mile they advanced toward the west."

Early in February, Eisenhower discussed with Bradley the
problem of avoiding an accidental clash in closing head-on with
the Russians. The two Americans agreed that prearranged recognition signals were not likely to work; they had even less faith
in the use of radio contact because of the language barrier.
What they needed was a visible geographic line of demarcation.
At the time of the conversation, the Russians were closing to
the Oder-Neisse line, SHAEF forces to the Rhine. The only
major river between them was the Elbe, which ran north and
south to Magdeburg, where it bent to the east. South of Magdeburg the Mulde River ran on nearly straight south to the Czech
border. It could be used to continue the boundary. Eisenhower,
from then on, had it in the back of his mind to make the Elbe-

18. In writing about the Normandy campaign, Bradley later declared, "It was partly this fear of running head-on into a single British
division at Falaise that had induced me to halt Patton's forces at
Argentan." In February, 1945, with one hundred times as many men
in a huge area, Bradley "shuddered at the prospect of a collision that
might easily flare into a fight." Bradley, *A Soldier's Story*, 531.

Mulde the demarcation line. It was an optimistic thought, for his forces were 250 miles or more from the Elbe while the Russians were within 100 miles; in Bradley's words, "the Elbe River line looked almost hopelessly beyond the reach of our Allied forces." [19]

Getting agreement on a stop line proved extraordinarily complex. Soviet, British, and United States airmen had been trying to work out solutions to the problems of bomb lines since June, 1944, with little success. On the ground the matter was even more difficult, because, in addition to such problems as language barriers and the absence of direct wire communication, there were the questions of the nature of lines of demarcation, procedure to follow when contact was imminent, withdrawal of various troops to their proper zones of occupation, and the probable necessity of having to advance beyond an agreed line of demarcation for emergency military purposes.[20] There was no effective liaison between the advancing forces, for although the Russians had some political contact with the Western Allies the Soviet government had consistently refused to allow the British and Americans to gain any significant knowledge of the Red Army's military plans and operations. The United States and Great Britain maintained military missions in Moscow, but until Eisenhower began his direct communication with Stalin the military missions merely passed on general information of SHAEF's operations; the information the West received through the missions was infinitesimal.

In view of all these problems and, more important, in view of the rapidly changing military situation, Eisenhower knew it was obviously impractical to make any definite proposals on boundaries until he had a better idea as to where the two sides would actually meet. General agreements were, however, imperative. On April 5, therefore, he proposed that "both fronts should be free to advance until contact is imminent." Stop lines might then be worked out by local commanders on the spot.

19. *Ibid.*, 532–33.
20. Pogue, *The Supreme Command,* 461.

Since this would probably bring the West into the Russian zone, he further proposed that, subject to operational necessity, either side would withdraw into its own zone at the request of the other.[21]

The British, just recovering from their shock over the telegram to Stalin, were furious. Churchill felt that Eisenhower's proposal would throw away the best bargaining point the West would hold at the end of the war. He most definitely wanted Allied troops within the Russian zone when the Germans surrendered, and he did not want them pulled out until he was certain Stalin would give something in return.[22] He insisted that questions of withdrawal from the Russian zone were governmental, not military matters, and had the British Chiefs of Staff suggest to the Joint Chiefs of Staff that Eisenhower be directed that "On cessation of operations our respective armies will stand fast until they receive orders from their Governments." [23]

The business of holding the other side's territory for trading purposes, however, could work two ways, as the United States State Department was quick to see. Officials of the European and Russian Affairs Divisions declared "that for governments to direct movement of troops definitely indicated *political* action and that *such movements should remain a military consideration* at least until SHAEF is dissolved and the ACC [Allied Control Commission] is set up." The State Department feared that the British proposal might send the Russians racing over Germany in an attempt to acquire as many square miles as possible before the war ended. Officials in the War Department were thankful for this interpretation of the British proposal because it indicated that the Department of State preferred "a

21. *Ibid.,* 465.
22. What Churchill wanted to trade was the Western occupied areas of the Russian zone for American and British entry into Berlin. In addition, the Red Army was probably going to overrun Austria, which had not been divided; Churchill wanted to make sure the West got into Austria and the best way to do so, he felt, was by trading. There was further the food problem discussed above in Chapter Two, Note 11.
23. Ehrman, *Grand Strategy,* 152.

straight military solution to the problem." [24]

The British Chiefs of Staff and the Joint Chiefs of Staff directed Eisenhower to get an agreement with the Russians that would allow both sides to advance until contact was imminent. Division of responsibility would then be settled by army group commanders. The Russians were suspicious of the proposal, fearing that the West was trying to redraw the zonal boundaries, and demanded that Eisenhower clarify that point. He assured the Red Army leaders that these arrangements were tactical only, and on April 15 agreement was reached. The Combined Chiefs of Staff then instructed Eisenhower to make no major withdrawals without consulting his superiors. The policy was finally clear. [25]

However, the question of where to stop was not; even with agreement reached, Eisenhower could not just have his troops rushing forward until they bumped into the Russians. He attempted to work out a system of signals and markings through which the two sides could identify themselves and avoid firing on each other, but no one had much faith in them. On April 21, therefore, Eisenhower told the Military Missions to Moscow to tell the Soviets that he intended to stop on the Elbe-Mulde line. Thereafter he would turn his forces north and south. The Russians almost immediately agreed. [26]

One last boundary problem remained to be settled with the Russians. As April drew to an end, Eisenhower's forces were overrunning southern Germany. Patton's Third Army had reached the Czech frontier and was preparing to move into Austria. The British Chiefs of Staff, at Churchill's urging, told the Joint Chiefs of Staff that the West could derive remarkable political advantages by liberating Prague and as much of Czechoslovakia as possible. They felt Eisenhower should not move to-

24. Pogue, *The Supreme Command,* 465.
25. *Ibid.,* 466; Ehrman, *Grand Strategy,* 152–60.
26. Pogue, *The Supreme Command,* 467. The first link-up came on April 25 at Torgau on the Elbe River; others followed rapidly along the entire front. The line did not apply in the north, where 21st Army Group did cross the Elbe. There were no major incidents.

ward Prague if it would interfere with his operations in the
Baltic and Austria, but if he could do all three together it could
lead to fruitful results.[27] Marshall passed the suggestion along
to Eisenhower on April 28, then added his own comment:
"Personally and aside from all logistic, tactical or strategical
implication I would be loath to hazard American lives for purely
political purposes."[28]

In his reply Eisenhower indicated that his main concern
coincided with Marshall's—a rapid termination of the war. He
would continue to emphasize the drive to Lübeck to cut off the
Germans in Norway and Denmark; the southern objective
would remain Linz and the National Redoubt, which would
make it impossible for the Germans to consolidate a defensive
position there. The Red Army, he said, was in a perfect position
to clean out Czechoslovakia and would certainly reach Prague
before his forces could. Eisenhower assured Marshall, "I shall
not attempt any move I deem militarily unwise merely to gain a
political prize unless I receive specific orders from the Combined Chiefs of Staff." Given Marshall's attitude, it was hardly
likely that the Combined Chiefs of Staff would intervene; in fact
they never even discussed the question.[29]

They did not because the Joint Chiefs of Staff did not wish
to and the British Chiefs of Staff knew it would be fruitless.
From the middle of April on, the British Chiefs of Staff confined
themselves to "noting" or "approving" Eisenhower's actions.
This was because they felt they had no choice; the argument
over the original telegram to Stalin and the central thrust had
clearly shown the limits of their influence and left no doubt of
the Joint Chiefs' determination to leave Eisenhower complete

27. Czechoslovakia had not been divided into occupation zones. It
was assumed that the country would regain its independence upon liberation. Austria, on the other hand, would be split off from Germany and
occupied. The zones for Austria, however, had not been decided upon.

28. Marshall to Eisenhower, April 28, Eisenhower Mss., Box 53,
quoted in Pogue, *The Supreme Command,* 468.

29. Eisenhower to Marshall, April 29, Eisenhower Mss., Box 53,
quoted in *ibid.,* 468–69.

freedom of action.[30]

Above the British Chiefs of Staff, however, the head of the British government did not feel hampered. He could appeal beyond the Joint Chiefs of Staff to the President (by this time Harry S Truman), and Churchill felt so strongly about Prague that he decided to do so. On April 30 he told Truman that American liberation of Prague would make a great difference in the postwar situation, for if the Red Army took the city Czechoslovakia would follow Yugoslavia into the communist camp. "Of course, such a move by Eisenhower must not interfere with his main operations against the Germans," Churchill added, "but I think the highly important political consideration mentioned above should be brought to his attention." [31]

The day Truman received Churchill's message, he also saw Eisenhower's proposal for future operations. The Supreme Commander reiterated that he intended to hold along the 1937 frontiers of Czechoslovakia while advancing to the general area of Linz. Later he might advance into Czechoslovakia to the line Pilsen-Karlsbad. Truman told Churchill, "This meets with my approval," and made it clear that, like his Joint Chiefs of Staff, he did not propose to interfere with Eisenhower. On May 3 the Russians told Eisenhower they too approved of his plans.[32] The next day, as German resistance in the south crumbled, Eisenhower told Bradley to send the 12th Army Group over the frontier. He then informed the Russians and added that he would be willing to advance beyond the Pilsen-Karlsbad line. On May 5, Marshal Antonov, Chief of Staff of the Red Army, replied. He did not want Eisenhower to move beyond the Pilsen-Karlsbad line and asked him, in order to avoid possible confusion, "not to move the Allied forces in Czechoslovakia east of the originally intended line." He added, significantly, that the

30. Ehrman, *Grand Strategy,* 160.

31. Feis, *Churchill, Roosevelt, and Stalin,* 610; Churchill, *Triumph and Tragedy,* 506; Wilmot, *Struggle for Europe,* 704.

32. Military Mission Moscow to Eisenhower, May 3, Eisenhower Mss., Box 53, quoted in Feis, *Churchill, Roosevelt, and Stalin,* 611; Wilmot, *Struggle for Europe,* 705.

Soviets had stopped their advance to the lower Elbe east of the line Wisman-Schwerin-Doemitz at Eisenhower's request. "We hope that General Eisenhower in turn will comply with our wishes relative to the advance of his forces in Czechoslovakia." [33]

Eisenhower agreed, even though the Czech partisans had meanwhile taken control of Prague and, under attack from the Germans, appealed to him for aid. On May 7 Churchill wired Eisenhower, "I am hoping that your plan does not inhibit you to advance to Prague if you have troops and do not meet the Russians earlier. I thought you did not mean to tie yourself down if you had the troops and the country was empty." [34] By then, however, events were moving too fast; Eisenhower was busy at Reims arranging for the German surrender, the Red Army was rushing into Czechoslovakia, and it was apparent already that American troops would be needed on the Austrian-Yugoslavian border to exert a restraining influence on the unruly Marshal Tito. Eisenhower left Prague to the Russians.

Years later, following the Communist take-over in Czechoslovakia, it was commonly asserted that Eisenhower's failure to take Prague led to this disaster. The charge was both unfair and wrong. The Americans had occupation forces in Czechoslovakia as long as the Russians did. The Communists came to power in Czechoslovakia as a result of an internal upheaval, long after the Red Army had departed from the country. It is true that at the time of the coup the Russians had troops on the Czech border, but so did the Americans.

Eisenhower's reasons for ignoring Czechoslovakia were twofold. Politics played a role. "When I directed Patton to shove hard to the south-east," Eisenhower later recalled, "I told him that the division of Germany had already been decided and zones of occupation delineated. This was not true of Austria

33. Military Mission Moscow to Eisenhower, May 5, Eisenhower Mss., Box 53, quoted in Pogue, *The Supreme Command*, 469; Ehrman, *Grand Strategy*, 159.

34. Churchill to Eisenhower, May 7, Eisenhower Mss., Box 13, quoted in Churchill, *Triumph and Tragedy*, 507.

and I was anxious to get as much of the latter country as possible." [35] This did not mean that Eisenhower was suddenly placing political above military considerations; it did mean that when political windfalls might accrue as a result of military moves, he was glad enough to take them. And the overriding consideration in Eisenhower's decision to move south into Austria was the same one that had led him to move south when his troops reached the Elbe—the fear of prolonged German resistance in the mountains.

35. Private communication to author, author's possession.

5

Could Eisenhower Have Taken Berlin?

~~~~~~

BY THE MIDDLE OF MARCH, Eisenhower's troops had closed to the Rhine River. Montgomery, in the north, was closest to Berlin, and he was 250 miles away. Eisenhower had a strong logistical position, based on his major port of Antwerp, and his lines of communication up to the Rhine were in good shape. Once his forces crossed the river, however, they would have to depend upon what could be air-dropped to them plus what they could carry. It would take time to build railroad and truck bridges across the Rhine (the Germans hardly could be expected to leave any bridges intact, and except for the Ludendorff Bridge at Remagen they did not—and even the Ludendorff Bridge was soon destroyed by German attacks); once over, SHAEF would have to depend upon the roads, for Allied air forces had torn up the railroad tracks inside Germany. Eisenhower planned to go all-out once across the river, but he knew his offensive was going to encounter immense logistical problems. The Russians, meanwhile, were building up large amounts of supplies and equipment on the Oder-Neisse line, 33 miles from Berlin.

On March 27, Montgomery had both British Second and U.S. Ninth Armies across. In addition Hodges had a major bridgehead at Remagen, while Patton had another between Mainz and Oppenheim. The encirclement of the Ruhr was under way. At a press conference that day, a reporter asked Eisenhower, "Who do you think will be into Berlin first, the Russians or us?" "Well," Eisenhower replied, "I think mileage alone ought to make them do it. After all they are thirty-three miles and we are two hundred and fifty. I wouldn't want to make any prediction. They have a shorter race to run, although they are faced by the bulk of the German forces." [1]

At the end of March, Eisenhower discussed with Bradley his alternatives. Bradley pointed out that even if the 21st Army Group reached the Elbe before Zhukov crossed the Oder, fifty miles of lowlands separated the Elbe from Berlin. Montgomery would have to advance through an area studded with lakes, criss-crossed with streams, and interlaced with occasional canals. Eisenhower asked Bradley for an estimate on the cost of taking Berlin. About 100,000 casualties, Bradley replied. "A pretty stiff price to pay for a prestige objective, especially when we've got to fall back and let the other fellow take over." Later, after the war, Bradley succumbed to the myth that the British had displayed remarkable political skill while the Americans demonstrated an amazing lack of sophistication. "I could see no political advantage in the capture of Berlin that would offset the need for quick destruction of the German army on our front," he wrote. Then he added what has become perhaps the most quoted sentence of the whole Berlin story: "As soldiers we looked naively on this British inclination to complicate the war with political foresight and non-military objectives." [2]

The truth is that Montgomery and the British advocated an attempt for Berlin as a military move, and Eisenhower rejected it on those grounds. Both at the time and later, those who maintained that Eisenhower should have tried have been extremely hazy on what the political profit would have been. Furthermore, although there was no certainty that the 21st Army Group could have made it to Berlin before the Red Army, it did seem obvious to SHAEF that, if the attempt were made, the Germans elsewhere, left alone, would strengthen their defenses and thus delay the end of the war. That clearly would have risked enormous political, as well as obvious military, consequences. Brad-

1. Butcher, *My Three Years With Eisenhower,* 788.
2. Bradley, *A Soldier's Story,* 535–36.

ley, in short, was being less than fair to himself and to his superior.

Eisenhower decided against making the attempt, at least with 21st Army Group, and Montgomery's forces headed north, towards Lübeck. On April 1, elements of U.S. First and Ninth Armies linked up west of Paderborn. Now those troops of the two armies not involved in reducing the Ruhr pocket (18 divisions undertook the task) were free to turn east, as was the entire U.S. Third Army. By April 4, two corps of Ninth Army were on the Weser River, while Patton's Third Army had troops in Kassel and Mühlhausen. The German position was desperate. They had one army group in Holland, which the Allies were, for fighting purposes, ignoring. The First Parachute Army was near Bremen; the Eleventh Army was cut off in the Harz mountains; the Seventh Army was on the Czechoslovakian border, and two other armies protected Austria. The men were short of everything, had practically no mobility, and they were confused. Communications were in a shambles. Orders did not go out, or if they did were not received, or, if received, made no sense because the High Command had only a foggy idea of what was going on at the front. Individual units were still fighting fiercely, but there was no coherent defense.

During the week of April 4–11, the Americans rushed eastward, delayed more by terrain and traffic jams than by German opposition. They made 30 miles a day in a campaign that brought out the best qualities of the American soldier. Eisenhower's feeling that Bradley's troops would give him a pell-mell pursuit proved well founded.

General William H. Simpson's Ninth Army, which skirted the northern edge of the Harz Mountains and was therefore held up least by terrain, moved fastest. On April 11 his spearheads reached the Elbe River. The final Russian drive for Berlin had not yet begun, and the Americans were within 50 miles of the city.

Suddenly what had appeared unobtainable since at least the Battle of the Bulge was seemingly within Eisenhower's grasp.

NORTH SEA

BALTIC SEA

DENMARK

Lübeck

Hamburg

2nd **RUSSIAN** ROKOSSOVSKI

WEICHSEL HEINRICI

H BLASKOWITZ

Bremen

POLAND

1st **RUSSIAN** ZHUKOV

NETHERLANDS

Elbe R.

BERLIN ★

Oder R.

RDAM

CANADIAN 1st

BRITISH 2nd

Magdeburg

CENTER SCHOERNER

1st **UKRAINIAN** KONEV

U.S. 9th

Paderborn

O B WEST KESSELRING Dessau

st A.G. TGOMERY

B MODEL

Rhine R.

U.S. 1st

Neisse R.

Elbe R.

h A.G. ADLEY

Bonn

Leipzig

Kassel

Mulde R.

Dresden

4th **UKRAINIAN** YEREMENKO

GIUM

Remagen Koblenz

U.S. 3rd

Karlsbad

LUXEMBOURG

Frankfurt

PRAGUE

Mainz

Main R.

U.S. 7th

G HAUSER

Pilsen

Rhine R.

GERMANY

CZECHOSLOVAKIA

A.G. ERS

SOUTH WOEHLER

FRENCH 1st

2nd **UKRAINIAN** MALINOVSKI

WESTERN FRONT LINE

Linz

NCE

Munich

Berchtesgaden

AUSTRIA

SWITZERLAND

EASTERN FRONT LINE

HE POSITION APRIL 4, 1945

ITALY

25   50   100

Scale of Miles

Simpson felt he had the momentum to keep right on going and get to Berlin before the Russians. He thought he could do it and asked Eisenhower's permission to try. Meanwhile he pushed bridgeheads across the Elbe, one north of Magdeburg on April 12 and another south of Magdeburg a day later. The one to the north was wiped out on April 14, but the one to the south held.

Still, Simpson thought he could make it. Eisenhower was not sure and in any case thought he had more important tasks. On April 14 he decided to stop at the Elbe and clean up his flanks, driving in the north to Lübeck and in the south to the Danube River valley. Once these operations were complete, if the opportunity was still there, he would try for Berlin.

Early the next morning, April 14, Bradley called Simpson on the telephone. The 12th Army Group Commander said he had something important to tell Simpson and wanted to say it in person. He would fly right over. Simpson met Bradley at the airfield. Bradley told Simpson to pull back across the Elbe. Simpson said he could be in Berlin in a day; Bradley replied that these were Eisenhower's orders.[3]

Simpson, bitterly disappointed, fought his emotions, finally gave in and issued the necessary orders. Nothing ever shook him from the belief that the only thing standing between Ninth Army and Berlin was a wide-open autobahn.[4] That, and something else. In the words of a military writer who agrees with Simpson, "There was nothing between him and Hitler except Eisenhower."[5]

On the same day that Bradley passed his orders on to Simpson, Eisenhower cabled Marshall to explain his thinking. After informing the Chief of Staff of his decision to hold on the Elbe, he said that not only were the Baltic and Bavarian objectives more important than the capital but that to plan for an immediate effort against Berlin "would be foolish in view of the relative

---

3. Toland, *The Last 100 Days,* 385; Ryan, *The Last Battle,* 333.
4. See Simpson's letter in the *New York Times Book Review,* June 19, 1966.
5. Toland, *The Last 100 Days,* 386.

situation of the Russians and ourselves . . . While it is true we have seized a small bridgehead over the Elbe, it must be remembered that only our spearheads are up to that river; our center of gravity is well back of there." [6]

When Simpson's spearheads reached the Elbe, not much more than fifty miles from Berlin, the Russians were still thirty-three miles from the city. The Russians had had two months in which to build up their strength while Eisenhower's men had just covered 250 miles in two weeks. The American center of gravity was indeed far back. No one, on either side, could have sustained an offensive of this scope and magnitude beyond the Elbe. Modern armies are unable to live off the countryside, and their means of transportation cannot forage for themselves. The armies of World War II were totally dependent on gasoline, a new phenomenon in the history of war. They ordinarily reached their limit after a 200-to-250-mile advance. This happened to the Germans in Russia in 1941, to the Russians in their 1944 offensive, and to the Western Allies in September, 1944. It happened to Eisenhower's forces in April, 1945. As one example of the problems involved in a headlong advance, Eisenhower's armies had left the fighter strips so far behind that airplanes had to carry reserve gasoline tanks on their wings just to keep up with the troops. They left their bombs behind.

The Americans reached the Elbe on April 11. They had one small bridgehead, were faced by one weak German army, and had a number of water barriers between them and Berlin. American strength in the area was not much more than 50,000 men, with little artillery. There were a few reinforcements available in the area, but to supply a drive beyond the Elbe Eisenhower would have had to devote to it nearly his entire air transport.[7]

6. Eisenhower to Marshall, April 15, Eisenhower Mss., Box 53, quoted in Pogue, "Decision to Halt," *op. cit.*, 487.

7. Wilmot, Eisenhower's most competent critic, agrees with the Supreme Commander's decision, although he believes that mistakes were made and insists that Montgomery could have made it if Eisenhower had given him proper support earlier in April. By the middle of the month, however, Wilmot feels that the logistical difficulties (which he

The Russians, fifteen miles closer to Berlin, had two solid bridgeheads, 1,250,000 men, and 22,000 pieces of artillery. They were faced by two weak German armies and had flat, dry land between them and Berlin.

By chance, America's most observant and expert combat historian, General S.L.A. Marshall, was with Simpson's spearheads on the Elbe River. On April 15 he got together with General Raymond S. McLain, commanding the XIX Corps, which was leading the way for Ninth Army. Marshall and McLain analyzed the situation. XIX Corps was spread out all over the countryside, its rear 150 miles from its front, with Germans attacking it on both flanks and the front. McLain concluded that at best he could get a few patrols into the outskirts of Berlin by the time the Russians had the city. Marshall agreed.[8]

There is one other factor. In the haze of speculation over the question, "Could they have made it?," the participants to the debate assume that the Russians would have acted exactly as they did no matter what the Americans undertook. Those who insist that Simpson could have taken Berlin make their strongest argument by concentrating on the dating of events. Simpson first crossed the Elbe on April 12; the Russians started their offensive for Berlin on April 16, reached the city on April 22, and completed its capture on May 2. Put another way, there were three weeks available to Ninth Army after it reached the Elbe, 50 miles from Berlin, before the Russians captured the entire city.

says were of Eisenhower's own making) were too great to be overcome. Bradley's forces were spread out on a 250-mile front and he had lost the capacity to concentrate the forces Simpson needed. The Americans only had eight divisions north of the Harz Mountains on the direct road to Berlin. The Allied Expeditionary Force had neither the strength nor the logistical capacity to make it to Berlin. *Struggle for Europe,* 695.

8. See Marshall's reviews of Toland, *The Last 100 Days,* in *New York Times Book Review,* February 13, 1966, and of Ryan, *The Last Battle,* in *ibid.,* March 27, 1966. Marshall thought McLain's reading of the situation was so self-evident that he did not bother to record the conclusion. In reviewing Toland's and Ryan's claims, Marshall has categorically denied that Ninth Army could have made it to Berlin.

NORTH SEA

DENMARK

BALTIC SEA

Lübeck

Hamburg

Bremen

**2nd
RUSSIAN**
ROKOSSOVSKI

POLAND

**1st
RUSSIAN**
ZHUKOV

WEICHSEL
HEINRICI

BERLIN ★

Elbe R.

Oder R.

**CANADIAN
1st**

BRITISH 2nd

Weser R.

U.S. 9th

12th A.G.
BRADLEY

Paderborn

Magdeburg

Dessau

CENTER
SCHOERNER

**1st
UKRANIAN**
KONEV

NETHERLANDS

ERDAM

Neisse R.

Kassel

U.S. 1st

Leipzig

Elbe R.

Mulde R.

21st A.G.
MONTGOMERY

Rhine R.

Bonn
Remagen
Koblenz

Dresden

**4th
UKRANIAN**
YEREMENKO

IUM

Frankfurt

Mainz

U.S. 3rd

Karlsbad

PRAGUE ★

UXEMBOURG

Rhine R.

Main R.

Pilsen

GERMANY

CZECHOSLOVAKIA

U.S. 7th

SOUTH
WOEHLER

6th A.G.
DEVERS

**2nd
UKRANIAN**
MALINOVSKI

FRENCH 1st

Linz

**WESTERN
FRONT
LINE**

Munich
Berchtesgaden

AUSTRIA

NCE

*EASTERN
FRONT*
LINE

SWITZERLAND

ITALY

**HE POSITION
APRIL 16, 1945**

25   50   100

Scale of Miles

The assumption Eisenhower's critics make is that the Russian timing would have been the same even if Simpson had pushed on for Berlin. It is strange that they make such an assumption so easily, since they also maintain that Stalin was fighting a political war and that he was determined to get Berlin first. Both assumptions cannot be correct. If Stalin was so set on Berlin, surely he would have pushed forward the start of his offensive once he saw Simpson's men heading for Berlin. And while Simpson could have started, at the very most, 50,000 men for Berlin, Stalin had 1,250,000 ready to go—and they had been gathering supplies and regrouping on the Oder-Neisse line for two months.

Simpson was not alone in thinking that Berlin was worth a try. On April 16, after learning of Eisenhower's plans, the British Chiefs of Staff suggested to the Combined Chiefs of Staff that they direct Eisenhower to take any opportunity to advance to Berlin. Churchill agreed with the position his chiefs took. The next day, Eisenhower flew to London and had a conference with the Prime Minister. The Supreme Commander convinced Churchill of the soundness of his views, and shortly after the meeting Churchill wired his foreign minister, who was in the United States. "It would seem that the Western Allies are not immediately in a position to force their way into Berlin," Churchill declared. "The Russians have two and a half million troops [*sic*] on the section of the front opposite that city. The Americans have only their spearheads, say twenty-five divisions [*sic*], which are covering an immense front and are at many points engaged with the Germans."

In a statement that reflected Eisenhower's views, Churchill went on to say that it was "most important" that Montgomery take Lübeck as soon as possible. Eisenhower had given 21st Army Group an American corps to strengthen Montgomery's attack. "Our arrival at Lübeck before our Russian friends from Stettin would save a lot of argument later on," the Prime Minister said. "There is no reason why the Russians should occupy Denmark, which is a country to be liberated and to have its sovereignty restored. Our position at Lübeck, if we get it, would be decisive in this matter." As indeed it was. Churchill also agreed with Eisenhower's decision to push on south of Stuttgart to capture the German atomic research facilities.[9]

The British Chiefs of Staff now stood completely alone, and they caved in. On April 18 they approved of Eisenhower's plans, and on the 21st he informed the Russians that he did not intend to move beyond the Elbe.[10] The Russians could take Berlin whenever they pleased.

Did it matter? In the long run, certainly not. In the short run, probably not. Still, those who feel that Simpson (or Montgomery) could have made it contend that it made a momentous difference. George Patton expressed this view as well as anyone. On the day Simpson reached the Elbe, April 11, Eisenhower had dinner with Patton. Afterwards, when they were alone, Eisenhower told Patton of his plans to clean up his flanks. "From a tactical point of view," Eisenhower added, "it is highly inadvisable for the American Army to take Berlin and I hope political influence won't cause me to take the city. It has no tactical or strategic value and would place upon the American forces the burden of caring for thousands and thousands of Germans displaced persons and Allied prisoners of war."

"Ike, I don't see how you figure that out," Patton replied. "We had better take Berlin, and quick—and on to the Oder!"

Later, at his headquarters, Patton again urged Eisenhower to try for Berlin. He said Simpson could take the city in forty-eight hours. "Well," Eisenhower asked, "who would want it?"

The Third Army commander put his hands on Eisenhower's shoulders and said, "I think history will answer that question for you." [11] Patton's romanticism, the influence of the Civil War on his mentality, was never more evident.

Montgomery seldom agreed with Patton, but he did on this

9. Churchill, *Triumph and Tragedy*, 515.
10. Ehrman, *Grand Strategy*, 148–49.
11. Quoted from the diary of Patton's G-3, General Hobart Gay, in Toland, *The Last 100 Days*, 371.

point. "The Americans could not understand that it was of little avail to win the war strategically if we lost it politically," he said later. "Because of this curious viewpoint we suffered accordingly from VE-Day onwards, and are still so suffering. War is a political instrument; once it is clear that you are going to win, political considerations must influence its further course. It became obvious to me in the autumn of 1944 that the way things were being handled was going to have repercussions far beyond the end of the war; it looked to me then as if we were going to 'muck it up.' I reckon we did." [12] Montgomery is saying that Eisenhower should have made a political decision that would have amounted to a change in high policy and raced the Russians to Berlin. What the West would have done with the city afterwards he does not make clear.

By battering their way into Berlin, the Russians suffered heavy casualties (the exact number is in dispute: it was probably in excess of the 100,000 Bradley feared).[13] Two months later they gave up to the West over half the city they had captured at such an enormous price. At the cost of not a single life, Great Britain and the United States had their sectors in Berlin. They have been there ever since.

And, more important, on May 5 the military resistance of Germany came to a complete end. As General Smith put it, "instead of wasting time and lives on ruined Berlin, the Allies had put an end to all German resistance in thirty-three climactic days by the only means the Nazis would accept. This . . . last great decision by the Supreme Commander insured the destruction of Hitler's armies in the West." [14]

12. Montgomery, *Memoirs*, 297.

13. Herbert Feis points out that they gained "the first somber sense of triumph, the first awesome sight of the ruins, the first parades under the pall of smoke." *Churchill, Roosevelt, and Stalin*, 609.

14. Smith, *Eisenhower's Six Great Decisions*, 184.

Appendices

Appendix A

The Telegrams

Churchill, *Triumph and Tragedy,* 463–67

Prime Minister to General Eisenhower   31 Mar. 45

Very many thanks. It seems to me personally that if the enemy's resistance does not collapse the shifting of the main axis of advance so much farther to the southward and the withdrawal of the Ninth U.S. Army from the Twenty first Army Group may stretch Montgomery's front so widely that the offensive role which was assigned to him may peter out. I do not know why it would be an advantage not to cross the Elbe. If the enemy's resistance should weaken, as you evidently expect and which may well be fulfilled, why should we not cross the Elbe and advance as far eastward as possible? This has an important political bearing, as the Russian armies of the South seem certain to enter Vienna and overrun Austria. If we deliberately leave Berlin to them, even if it should be in our grasp, the double event may strengthen their conviction, already apparent, that they have done everything.

2. Further, I do not consider myself that Berlin has yet lost its military and certainly not its political significance. The fall of Berlin would have a profound psychological effect on German resistance in every part of the Reich. While Berlin holds out great masses of Germans will feel it their duty to go down fighting. The idea that the capture of Dresden and junction with the Russians there would be a superior gain does not commend itself to me. The parts of the German Government departments which have moved south can very quickly move southward again. But while Berlin remains under the German flag it can-

not, in my opinion, fail to be the most decisive point in Germany.

3. Therefore I should greatly prefer persistence in the plan on which we crossed the Rhine, namely, that the Ninth U.S. Army should march with the Twenty-first Army Group to the Elbe and beyond Berlin. This would not be in any way inconsistent with the great central thrust which you are now so rightly developing as the result of the brilliant operations of your armies south of the Ruhr. It only shifts the weight of one army to the northern flank.

Prime Minister to President Roosevelt   1 Apr. 45

You will have read the telegrams between the British Chiefs of Staff and their United States colleagues. I think there is some misunderstanding on both sides, which I am anxious to disperse without more ado.

2. We are very much obliged to the United States Chiefs of Staff for their paragraph which gives time for a reasonable interchange of views between our two Chiefs of Staff Committees.

3. I am however distressed to read that it should be thought that we wish in the slightest degree to discredit or lower the prestige of General Eisenhower in his increasingly important relations with the Russian commanders in the field. All we sought was a little time to consider the far-reaching changes desired by General Eisenhower in the plans that had been concerted by the Combined Chiefs of Staff at Malta and had received your and my joint approval. The British Chiefs of Staff were naturally concerned by a procedure which apparently left the fortunes of the British Army, which though only a third of yours still amounts to over a million men, to be settled without the slightest reference to any British authority. They also did not fully understand from General Eisenhower's message what actually was intended. In this we may be excused, because Gen-

eral Deane was similarly puzzled and delayed delivery of General Eisenhower's message to Stalin for twenty hours in order to ask for background. I am in full agreement in this instance with the procedure proposed by your Chiefs of Staff, and I am sorry we did not think of it ourselves.

4. At this point I wish to place on record the complete confidence felt by His Majesty's Government in General Eisenhower, our pleasure that our armies are serving under his command, and our admiration of the great and shining qualities of character and personality which he has proved himself to possess in all the difficulties of handling an Allied Command. Moreover, I should like to express to you, Mr. President, as I have already done orally in the field to General Eisenhower, my heartfelt congratulations on the glorious victories and advances by all the armies of the United States Centre in the recent battles on the Rhine and over it. . . .

5. Having dealt with and I trust disposed of these misunderstandings between the truest friends and comrades that ever fought side by side as allies, I venture to put to you a few considerations upon the merits of the changes in our original plans now desired by General Eisenhower. It seems to me the differences are small, and, as usual, not of principle but of emphasis. Obviously, laying aside every impediment and shunning every diversion, the Allied armies of the North and Centre should now march at the highest speed towards the Elbe. Hitherto the axis has been upon Berlin. General Eisenhower, on his estimate of the enemy's resistance, to which I attach the greatest importance, now wishes to shift the axis somewhat to the southward and strike through Leipzig, even perhaps as far south as Dresden. He withdraws the Ninth United States Army from the northern group of armies, and in consequence stretches its front southward. I should be sorry if the resistance of the enemy was such as to destroy the weight and momentum of the advance of the British Twenty-first Army Group and to leave them in an almost static condition along the Elbe when and if they reach it. I say quite frankly that Berlin remains of

high strategic importance. Nothing will exert a psychological effect of despair upon all German forces of resistance equal to that of the fall of Berlin. It will be the supreme signal of defeat to the German people. On the other hand, if left to itself to maintain a siege by the Russians among its ruins, and as long as the German flag flies there, it will animate the resistance of all Germans under arms.

6. There is moreover another aspect which it is proper for you and me to consider. The Russian armies will no doubt overrun all Austria and enter Vienna. If they also take Berlin will not their impression that they have been the overwhelming contributor to our common victory be unduly imprinted in their minds, and may this not lead them into a mood which will raise grave and formidable difficulties in the future? I therefore consider that from a political standpoint we should march as far east into Germany as possible, and that should Berlin be in our grasp we should certainly take it. This also appears sound on military grounds.

7. To sum up, the difference that might exist between General Eisenhower's new plans and those we advocated, and which were agreed upon beforehand, would seem to be the following, viz., whether the emphasis should be put on an axis directed on Berlin or on one directed on Leipzig and Dresden. This is surely a matter upon which a reasonable latitude of discussion should be allowed to our two Chiefs of Staff Committees before any final commitment involving the Russians is entered into.

8. I need hardly say that I am quite willing that this message, which is my own personal message to you and not a Staff communication, should be shown to General Marshall.

General Eisenhower to Prime Minister   1 Apr. 45

After reading your message dated yesterday I think you still have some misunderstanding of what I intend to do.

In the first place I repeat that I have not changed any plan. I made certain groupings of this force in order to cross the Rhine, with the main deliberate thrust in the north, isolate the Ruhr, and disrupt, surround, or destroy the Germans defending that area. This is as far as strategic objectives of this force have ever been approved by me, because obviously such a victory over the German forces in the West and such a blow to its industrial capacity would necessarily create new situations requiring study and analysis before the next broad pattern of effort could be accurately sketched.

The situation that is now developing is one that I have held before my Staff for more than a year as the one toward which we shall strive, namely, that our forces should be concentrating across the Rhine through avenues of Wesel and Frankfurt and situated roughly in a great triangle with the apex resting in the Kassel area. From there onward the problem was to determine the direction of the blow that would create the maximum disorganisation to the remaining German forces and the German power of resisting. I had never lost sight of the great importance of the drive to the northernmost coast, although your telegram did introduce a new idea respecting the political importance of the early attainment of particular objectives. I clearly see your point in this matter. The only difference between your suggestions and my plan is one of timing. .... In order to assure the success of each of my planned efforts, I concentrate first in the Centre to gain the position I need. As it looks to me now, the next move thereafter should be to have Montgomery cross the Elbe, reinforced as necessary by American troops, and reach at least a line including Lübeck on the coast. If German resistance from now on should progressively and definitely crumble you can see that there would be little if any difference in time between gaining central position and crossing the Elbe. On the other hand, if resistance tends to stiffen at all I can see that it is vitally necessary that I concentrate for each effort, and do not allow myself to be dispersed by attempting to do all these projects at once.

Quite naturally, if at any moment collapse should suddenly come about everywhere along the front we would rush forward, and Lübeck and Berlin would be included in our important targets.

Prime Minister to General Eisenhower   2 Apr. 45

Thank you again for your most kind telegram. . . . I am however all the more impressed with the importance of entering Berlin, which may well be open to us, by the reply from Moscow to you, which in paragraph 3 says, "Berlin has lost its former strategic importance." This should be read in the light of what I mentioned of the political aspects. I deem it highly important that we should shake hands with the Russians as far to the east as possible. . . .

4. The arrival of your additional information has largely allayed the anxieties of our Staffs, and they have telegraphed in this sense to their opposite numbers in Washington. You will, I am sure, make allowance for the fact that we had heard nothing at all about this either officially or from our Deputy [Air Chief Marshall Tedder, at Eisenhower's headquarters] until we saw your telegram to Stalin, and this telegram made them think that very large changes were proposed.

5. I regard all this business as smoothing itself down quite satisfactorily, though some correspondence is still proceeding between our Chiefs of Staff Committees.

6. Again my congratulations on the great developments. Much may happen in the West before the date of Stalin's main offensive.

Appendix B
Eisenhower's Directive

~~~~~~

Pogue, *Supreme Command*, 53–55

The Combined Chiefs of Staff directive
to General Eisenhower declared:

1. You are hereby designated as Supreme Allied Commander of the forces placed under your orders for operations
for the liberation of Europe from the Germans. Your title will
be Supreme Commander, Allied Expeditionary Force.

2. Task. You will enter the continent of Europe, and, in
conjunction with the other United Nations, undertake operations aimed at the heart of Germany and the destruction of her
armed forces. The date for entering the Continent is the month
of May 1944. After adequate channel ports have been secured,
exploitation will be directed to securing an area that will facili-
tate both ground and air operations against the enemy.

3. Notwithstanding the target date above, you will be prepared at any time to take immediate advantage of favorable circumstances, such as the withdrawal by the enemy on your front,
to effect a re-entry into the Continent with such forces as you
have available at the time; a general plan for this operation
when approved will be furnished for your assistance.

4. Command. You are responsible to the Combined Chiefs
of Staff and will exercise command generally in accordance with
the diagram at Appendix A. Direct communication with the
United States and British Chiefs of Staff is authorized in the interest of facilitating your operations and for arranging necessary
logistic support.

5. Logistics. In the United Kingdom the responsibility for
logistics organization, concentration, movement and supply of
forces to meet the requirements of your plan will rest with Brit-

105

ish Service Ministries so far as British Forces are concerned. So far as United States Forces are concerned, this responsibility will rest with the United States War and Navy Departments. You will be responsible for the co-ordination of logistical arrangements on the continent. You will also be responsible for co-ordinating the requirements of British and United States Forces under your command.

6. Co-ordination of operations of other Forces and Agencies. In preparation for your assault on enemy occupied Europe, Sea and Air Forces, agencies of sabotage, subversion and propaganda, acting under a variety of authorities, are now in action. You may recommend any variation in these activities which may seem to you desirable.

7. Relationship to United Nations Forces in other areas. Responsibility will rest with the Combined Chiefs of Staff for supplying information relating to operations of the forces of the U.S.S.R. for your guidance in timing your operations. It is understood that the Soviet forces will launch an offensive at about the same time as OVERLORD with the object of preventing the German forces from transferring from the Eastern to the Western front. The Allied Commander-in-Chief, Mediterranean Theater, will conduct operations designed to assist your operation, including the launching of an attack against the south of France at about the same time as OVERLORD. The scope and timing of his operations will be decided by the Combined Chiefs of Staff. You will establish contact with him and submit to the Combined Chiefs of Staff your views and recommendations regarding operations from the Mediterranean in support of your attack from the United Kingdom. The Combined Chiefs of Staff will place under your command the forces operating in Southern France as soon as you are in a position to assume such command. You will submit timely recommendations compatible with this regard.

8. Relationship with Allied Governments—the re-establishment of Civil Governments and Liberated Allied Territories and the administration of Enemy Territories. Further instructions will be issued to you on these subjects at a later date.

A Note on Sources

~~~~~~

THERE IS an enormous literature on World War II, one so vast that no individual can keep up with it. Still, some books are better than others. I discuss below those which I found most helpful.

Any serious student of the American role in World War II must begin his study by becoming thoroughly familiar with the official Army history, the *United States Army in World War II,* of which some seventy volumes have been published to date. Authors in the series are members of the Office of the Chief of Military History, working under the general editorship of, until 1958, Dr. Kent Roberts Greenfield and after 1958 under Dr. Stetson Conn. The series is divided into parts, of which the most important for the reader interested in Berlin are the volumes in "European Theater of Operations." As a whole, the series' defects are formal writing and occasionally too much detail. The positive features of the works far outweigh the shortcomings. The authors have full access to the record; all are trained professional historians; no official put any impediment in their path; their manuscripts, whenever possible, are reviewed by those who participated in the events, which review often led to the discovery of new information or to a fuller understanding of what had merely been glimpsed before.

On the Berlin question, a number of volumes in the series are useful. Aside from those dealing with operations in France and Germany, the reader should consult Roland G. Ruppenthal, *Logistical Support of the Armies,* Volume II (1959), Ray S. Cline, *Washington Command Post: The Operations Division* (1951), and Maurice Matloff, *Strategic Planning for Coalition Warfare, 1943–1944* (1959). Of primary importance for an understanding of Eisenhower's role is Forrest C. Pogue, *The Supreme Command* (1954), the history of SHAEF. Pogue's book is perhaps the finest volume in the entire series.

A useful addition to the series is a work edited by Dr. Greenfield, *Command Decisions* (1960). The volume contains articles written by historians in the Office of the Chief of Military History on crucial decisions of World War II. A number of these bear on operations in France and Europe; the most important is Dr. Pogue's "The Decision to Halt at the Elbe."

The official British history, *History of the Second World War, United Kingdom Military Series,* edited by J. R. M. Butler, differs from the American in a number of respects. It is better written, more concerned with high policy, and does not get bogged down in details. There are, unfortunately, no citations to documents. It is overall an excellent series, and a perusal of it is necessary to an understanding of the development of coalition warfare. Fortunately the work which deals most directly with the Berlin question is, like Pogue's, perhaps the best in the series. John Ehrman's *Grand Strategy: October 1944–August 1945* (1956), Volume VI in the series, is a magnificent book. As well as being a first-rate writer, Ehrman is a thinker with insight, one whose judgments always have to be respected.

A good supplement to the official histories are the memoirs of participants. On the whole the memoirs suffer from an absence of documentation and an occasional lapse into inaccuracy. They make up for this by supplying invaluable material on atmosphere, which is something more than mere "color" and includes the mood of the time and a glimpse into the conditions under which the men who made the decisions were working. Beyond this, the more outspoken memoir writers provide material on personal relationships not available elsewhere.

George Marshall did not write his memoirs (a gap which Pogue's forthcoming multi-volume biography will at least partly fill); neither, of course, did Roosevelt or Stalin. All the other major figures did. One begins with Churchill's *The Second*

World War. The sixth and last volume, *Triumph and Tragedy* (1953) deals with the issues covered in this book. Churchill's theme is "How the Great Democracies Triumphed, and so Were Able to Resume the Follies Which Had so Nearly Cost Them Their Life." He insists throughout the work that he saw the Cold War coming and tried to get the United States to follow him in adopting policies that would forestall Russian advances in central Europe and elsewhere. Churchill is especially valuable because he prints many important documents, even though he frequently deletes paragraphs without informing the reader. *Triumph and Tragedy* is, of course, great historical literature.

The British side of the story is continued in Brooke's and Montgomery's memoirs. Brooke's appear in an unusual form, as they were written by Sir Arthur Bryant. The chief source, however, was Brooke's personal diary, which Bryant quotes extensively, and Brooke went over the manuscript carefully. There are two volumes, *The Turn of the Tide 1939–1943* (1957) and *Triumph in the West* (1959). Brooke's diary gives an insider's view of the workings of the British Chiefs of Staff and of the problems of one who had intimate dealings with Churchill. His caustic comments about Eisenhower and the Americans reveal the prejudices under which he operated. The same is true of Montgomery; of his many works the most important is *The Memoirs of Field-Marshal Montgomery of Alamein* (1958), which has the bonus of reprinting a number of documents not available elsewhere. See also Francis de Guingand, *Operation Victory* (1947), by Montgomery's Chief of Staff. *The Memoirs of General Lord Ismay* (1960) are a good source and a delight to read.

The two most important American memoirs are Eisenhower's *Crusade in Europe* (1948) and Bradley's *A Soldier's Story* (1951). Bradley is much more outspoken than Eisenhower, much more willing to share his feelings about people—especially Montgomery—with the reader. *Crusade in Europe* is a straightforward account, extremely helpful for its details on the basis of decision-making but somewhat disappointing because of the absence of any discussion of personal relationships. True to his nature, Eisenhower either says something complimentary about his associates or does not mention them. Walter Bedell Smith's memoirs, *Eisenhower's Six Great Decisions* (1956), are disappointing because they are so self-effacing. Smith played a much larger role than he indicates. Still the reader should consult Chapter Six, "The Only Way it Could End." Finally, *I Was There* (1950), by William D. Leahy, Roosevelt's and Truman's personal chief of staff, is, while usually shallow, sometimes illuminating.

Harry C. Butcher's *My Three Years With Eisenhower* (1946), the diary of Eisenhower's personal aide, is not as useful on the final campaigns as it is for earlier stages of the war. Butcher took a position with SHAEF Public Relations in late 1944 and did not spend as much time with Eisenhower thereafter as he had earlier in the war. He does reprint the full text of Smith's press conference of April 21.

Of the many general histories of the war in Europe, the best remains Chester Wilmot, *The Struggle for Europe* (1952).Wilmot writes from a British point of view; his attitude towards Eisenhower and the Americans is close to that of Brooke. His work is detailed, accurate, thoughtful and easy to read.

On the European Advisory Commission and diplomacy in general, much the finest work is Herbert Feis, *Churchill, Roosevelt, Stalin: The War They Waged and the Peace They Sought* (1957). Feis is a careful historian whose great strengths are completeness and unquestioned accuracy. William M. Franklin, "Zonal Boundaries and Access to Berlin," *World Politics,* Volume XVI (October 1963), by a historian with the Department of State, is a good short history of the European Advisory Commission. On zones, see also Frederick Morgan, *Overture to Overlord* (1950). On alliance warfare in general, see the brilliant pamphlet by Gordon A. Craig, *Problems of Coalition Warfare: The Military Alliance Against Napoleon, 1813–1814* (1965).

Three recent works have dealt with the question of Berlin.

Rodney G. Minott, *The Fortress That Never Was* (1965), demonstrates conclusively that the National Redoubt was a myth, although Minott misjudges the effect that the Redoubt had on Eisenhower's strategy. John Toland's *The Last 100 Days* (1965) and Cornelius Ryan's *The Last Battle* (1966) cover the same ground in much the same fashion. Both have countless vignettes and flashbacks, both try to create unbearable suspense, both try to copy Bruce Catton's techniques. Toland and Ryan are extremely critical of Eisenhower's decision to halt at the Elbe and are certain that Simpson's troops could have reached Berlin before the Russians. The careful student should consult S. L. A. Marshall's reviews of Ryan (March 27, 1966) and Toland (February 13, 1966) in the *New York Times Book Review*. See also Stephen Ambrose, "Refighting the Last Battle —The Pitfalls of Popular History," *Wisconsin Magazine of History*, Volume XLIX (Summer, 1966).

I have seen the originals of all the Eisenhower, Marshall, Joint Chiefs of Staff, and Combined Chiefs of Staff material quoted in this work, and most of the Churchill messages. All citations, however, include the printed works in which the material may be found, mainly because the printed works are more readily available.

Index